If you have a smartphone, you've felt ... our phones too much, and we feel e... apps, we try to use our phones less, t... The problem is that we never address t... itual. If we want to form a new, healtl... to sever our unhealthy attachments – ...es. That's what T. J. Burdick helps us do in this fine boo... Through timeless spiritual practices you'll learn how to treat your phone prudently, as a tool and not an addictive slot machine. If you want to master your tech, and not the other way around, put down your device and read this book!

— **Brandon Vogt**, content director at Word on Fire Ministries

If left unchecked, technology addiction can be a major source of unhappiness, a drain on personal productivity, and a potential lure to sinfulness. In *Detached*, T. J. Burdick provides a systematic retreat approach to help us gain control over our devices and our own behavior. Based upon timeless truths of the Faith, this twenty-one-day retreat offers a helpful framework for placing our overly wired lives back into balance and well-being.

— **Lisa M. Hendey**, author of *The Grace of Yes*

Has your life become too phony? Are you so attached to your phone that you never feel at rest without it, while you neglect the family and friends who are attached to you, and the God who gave you all life? If you would seek to change your priorities and grow in a life of genuine happiness and holiness, then set aside that glowing rectangle for just a while and let T. J. Burdick guide you on the twenty-one-day retreat within the wise, warm pages of *Detached: Put Your Phone in Its Place*. Replete with startling scientific findings, humorous personal anecdotes, and penetrating insights of the Church and her saints, this book will withdraw you from worldly technological addiction and direct you toward appropriate use of the wonders of technology, as you advance toward greater intimacy with God, and reorient toward the people and things that truly matter the most.

— **Kevin Vost, Psy.D.,** author of *How to Think Like Aquinas*

Whether your relationship with your phone is under control or spiraling into chaos, you need this book. T. J. Burdick uses timeless wisdom and insight to steer you into a life where you are controlling your phone, not the other way around.

— **Sarah Reinhard**, author and blogger, SnoringScholar.com

All who desire true happiness will read *Detached* from T. J. Burdick. Many may be intimidated by the idea of a permanent hiatus from their phone and apps, but T. J. convincingly proves that it is possible with this thoroughly researched and shrewdly crafted approach to using phones in the right proportion and with the correct purpose.

— **Shaun McAfee**, author of *Reform Yourself!* and founder of EpicPew.com

DETACHED

Put Your Phone in Its Place

T. J. BURDICK

Our Sunday Visitor
www.osv.com
Our Sunday Visitor Publishing Division
Our Sunday Visitor, Inc.
Huntington, Indiana 46750

Our Sunday Visitor Publishing Division
Our Sunday Visitor, Inc.
200 Noll Plaza
Huntington, IN 46750
1-800-348-2440

ISBN: 978-1-68192-359-8 (Inventory No. T2048)
eISBN: 978-1-68192-360-4
LCCN: 2018950741

Cover design: Tyler Ottinger
Cover art: Shutterstock
Interior design: Chelsea Alt

PRINTED IN THE UNITED STATES OF AMERICA

To my children Sofía, Saraí, Santiago, and Michael,
who will vanquish far worse temptations in technology than I
could ever imagine.

TABLE OF CONTENTS

INTRODUCTION

Your phone is likely no more than ten feet away from you as you read this. Its presence alone changes the environment completely, doesn't it? In that tiny device there exists endless streams of intellectual stimulation, entertainment, communication, and cat pictures.

You have held that luminescent box in your hand and felt its power. You've come to understand that its strength is sometimes a necessary component to your day-to-day activities, a life force that draws you into its potential for efficiency, cooperation, productivity, and fun.

On the other hand, you've also felt the darkness of your relationship with that phone. You've witnessed its ability to entice you with mindlessness and vainglory. You've likely spent your free time (and some of your working hours) swiping and button pushing, texting and scrolling, binge-watching and game playing into the wee hours of the night, ignoring even your most loved ones in the process. Like Frodo and the Ring, you feel a special connection with your phone, one that you've come to realize is unhealthy at best, and addictive at worst.

You want more, don't you?

Since the dawn of the smartphone more than a decade ago, we have struggled to identify what our right relationship with technology should be. There are several books and studies that examine the effects of technology use from a secular viewpoint, but very few (if any) books address the spiritual effects of our screens. It is my theory that our devices, especially our phones, have led us to focus less on living happier, holier lives. You've likely felt that same spiritual confusion and unease, which is why you have picked up this book.

I wrote this book to help you, as the title indicates, detach yourself from your phone and put it in its proper place. Your phone should be helping you achieve the spiritual heights that God has intended for you, but at this point your phone is doing more to keep you from achieving his will for your life. This book will teach you how to detach yourself from your phone's addictive temptations, and ultimately move you toward living a life of heroic Christian virtue.

My Story

In 2009, my wife, Maribel, and I purchased smartphones for the first time. We were dirt poor. We had just come back from a year as international missionaries and, with only my income as a first-year teacher, we struggled to make ends meet.

We were accustomed to the old-school text and talk phones we had bought two years prior. Then one day my wife's phone quite literally blew up. Our cellphone provider made us an offer we couldn't refuse: Smartphones, surprisingly, were the cheapest replacement.

When we brought the devices into our home, however, the family dynamic changed. I've noticed that, at home, the reception waves flow from this lifeless bit of machinery into my soul and pull me away from many opportunities to fulfill my God-given role as a father. When with my kids, I'm "lol"-ing at the latest meme instead of making them laugh in real life with dad jokes. When my son asks me to read him a book, I tell him, "Just a minute while I finish this email and then we can read *Hop on Pop*." While my daughter climbs on my lap to offer a bowl of imaginary soup, my thumbs text a friend while I open my mouth wide without making the slightest bit of eye contact, and I swallow my guilt. It all came to a head when my third child, my first son, was coming into the world.

My wife Maribel, my mother, and I were in the hospital, where my wife's pain medication had made her fall asleep for the entire night. My son's birth would be delayed, and labor would be induced in a few hours when the doctor arrived.

Unable to sleep, I was alone in the dark hospital room anticipating my son's arrival with wonder and awe. But this was my third child, so I knew the drill; I'd have a long time before I was needed. So I drifted into the digital world. I sifted through my professional work first, responding to emails from clients and bosses. Then I began dabbling in texts, social media, email, games, and every app I could find. I lost myself in the electronic universe for hours during the stillness of the seemingly eternal night, leaving my body weary and my mind dull.

When the moment came for me to be the encouraging husband, the one who is supposed to comfort his wife and welcome his first son into the world, I found myself holding my wife with one hand and my iPhone with the other. All who were present — the nurses, the doctor, even my own mother — looked at me with shocked discontent. Oblivious to their stares, my own eyes were glued to God knows what was on my cellphone screen. I had already finished my necessary work three or four hours ago. I was being entertained by emptiness. Maribel then took her hand away from mine, looked deep into my eyes and said: "T. J., seriously? Can you put down your phone? I need you now. ALL of you."

In that moment I realized I was an addict. What kind of man chooses to distract himself from the birth of his son with meaningless entertainment? How disturbing it must have been for everyone who watched me stare blankly into a screen when I should have held my head up proudly as the father of a new and beautiful son. Yet, a few minutes later, there I was. There we were. All of us, including my son, whose first breaths I would have missed had my wife not called me back to reality. I turned off my phone for the rest of the day and became a daddy again.

As my family, home and work responsibilities grew, simultaneously technology advanced in quantity and quality. On those few occasions that Maribel and I were both well-rested and able to leave the house to go have some fun with our kids, I took a look around and saw endless streams of people with their heads buried in their phones. At the restaurant, young couples were not staring into one another's eyes in the rapture of young love; in their homes, families were not playing board games or reading books; on the playground, parents were not playing with their children. Everyone seemed to be ignoring everyone else, instead paying close attention to whatever was happening on their phones.

And today it continues.

Since my son's birth, I've longed to live a happy life, one that is fulfilling, satisfying, meaningful, and focused. To do so, I have had to learn how to live in a new way, a way that harnesses technology as a tool to build the good life I desire, not the distracted one I fell into long ago.

If you are still reading this book, that means that you desire to live the good life, too.

A Fair Warning

The method that I am proposing will not have you go the *Lord of the Rings* route by climbing to the top of Mount Doom and throwing your devices into a pit of molten lava (although that might be progress). On the contrary, our devices contain millions of ways to help us live healthier, happier, and more efficient lives.

There are numerous ways in which technology has advanced humanity. I personally have managed to grow my own business, publish several books, and connect with people through social media who have helped me grow into a successful writer, theologian, and entrepreneur. None of these would have been possible had I not learned how to use my screens as the powerful tools they were meant be.

The problem occurs when we put too much of our focus on the tool itself, when we become so attached to it that our lives become twisted and burdensome. The problem isn't the technology; the problem is the attachment we have to technology. This attachment is what needs to go, which requires that an individual have an actual desire to get rid of that attachment. If you do not have that desire, then this book will do nothing for you.

It is this attachment to technology that we will carry with us during these next twenty-one days and cast into the abyss. In other words, we won't sacrifice the good stuff that technology provides, but we will sacrifice its negative effects. Then we will be able to realize the potential of our personal excellence, which has its origin and final destination in full participation in the glory of Christ.

Jesus tells us, "The thief comes only to steal and kill and destroy; I have come that they may have life, and have it abundantly" (Jn 10:10). The thief that has come to steal and kill your soul is your phone. Detachment from your phone, then, is the first step toward living a life of happiness and holiness — a life of true abundance.

How This Retreat Works

Over the course of the next three weeks, you will be asked to read, reflect, and occasionally take action. The first two days are the most labor-intensive, as they involve the necessary scheduling and purging components of the retreat. During each day, you will spend time reading a meditation and reflecting on how technology fits into God's will for your life. Some days will take more time than others, but all have been designed to help you gradually strengthen your personal and spiritual life while decreasing the minutes you spend on your phone.

I've also created several free resources to help you as you make your retreat. At detachedlife.com you'll find tools including monitoring apps, instructions on how to remove apps and push notifications, social media overlays (to let your friends know you are on retreat), other tech detachment tips, interviews, and more.

I am thrilled that you have taken this first step toward detaching from your phone. May the next twenty-one days bear much fruit for your soul. I will be praying for you.

DAY 1

The System: Preparing to Detach

The goal of purging from your digital life is to install the systems that will guide you away from phone distractions toward actions that will make you truly happy. Although technology offers limitless ways to grow in happiness, you must first fortify your will through discipline if you want to achieve the highest possible degree of joy. You will only arrive at this level by developing the ability to deny yourself, take up your cross (or, in this case, your phone), and follow Jesus.

Trust me on this. I've read all the self-help books, completed all the social media fasts, deleted all the apps (and then downloaded them again), I've even downsized from smartphone to non-smartphone for a time in an effort to curb my technology addictions. While all of those certainly had positive effects, it was in the beauty and mystery of the Catholic faith that my technology addictions were finally kept at bay. I didn't need a twelve-step program or a digital detox retreat in the middle of the forest, miles away from a Wi-Fi signal. All I needed was the wisdom of Christendom which, for more than two thousand years, has taught us how to detach ourselves from worldly desires.

This book will systemically guide you through the wisdom of Mother Church. It will reveal to you what you are dealing with, what God wants from you, and what life can be like if you are willing to battle against the enemy of distraction and resist the temptation to use your phone in ways that do not advance sanctity.

As Christians, we've already been given countless lessons on how to detach ourselves from worldly desires. Every Gospel reading calls us to communion with Christ and not the worldly desires that tempt us; every Lent we sacrifice time, talent, and treasure as we await the joy of Easter; and every Advent we practice patience as we prepare our souls to receive the Christ Child on Christmas Day.

All of this "basic training" is built into our Christian lives. However, like a trained soldier going to war for the first time, we must dig ourselves a trench and hunker down. Before we can advance toward the goal of full detachment, we must learn to defend our interior castle by establishing a battle plan.

Here's what I recommend.

Evaluate Your Daily Schedule

The first step in the purge process is to take a close look at how you spend your days. This may seem like a trivial — or perhaps overwhelming — step, but it is a deeply important one for you to truly benefit from these twenty-one days.

Our habits define who we are. The amount of time we dedicate to our activities shows how much we love and value those things. Time and habits go hand in hand. Many people have good habits that help them achieve the happiness and holiness they desire. They have a consistent prayer life, spend time with loved ones, and enjoy hobbies and work because they have allotted the appropriate amount of time to those particular activities.

However, for many of us, our time and habits aren't always a perfect match. We tend to give more time to bad habits such as social media, gaming, online shopping, etc., than to the things that actually provide us with fulfillment. We see our holiness and our screen time like star-crossed lovers destined to be together at some point, but never knowing just how the two could coexist because we are unwilling to give up screen time in order to pursue God. Time and habits must first agree upon their final end, which is holiness, before they can be of any use to the other. So we must purge all that keeps the two from living a healthy relationship with each other.

The best way to achieve this harmony is to arrange your day based on your priorities. When family, friends, work, hobbies, and basic needs are given the proper amount of time needed to help you thrive, your habits become solidified into virtue and you are more able to love and be loved by others and by God. You become more closely connected to God, who provides you with clarity in your decision-making. Scheduling actually frees up time for yourself and others by eliminating everything that wastes your time. You then learn the value of every second of your day and are thus able to pray, work, rest, and enjoy life as it was meant to be enjoyed.

The Bible tells us that our God is a God "of peace" (1 Cor 14:33). As such we must organize our lives if we aspire to become one with him. Life is a gift from God, and you have the responsibility of living it to its fullest so that it will bear fruit for his kingdom. The first step is to carefully evaluate your daily schedule.

Creating a Daily Schedule

This may sound completely overwhelming — you have too many moving pieces in your day, there are too many unknown variables when you get up in the morning. Trust me, I know. At one point in my life I had four children five years old or younger, worked a full-time job, and somehow managed to find time to pursue a master's degree. Was I able to keep a schedule then? Not successfully, but at least I had the intention to place each of those nonnegotiable parts of my life into something that *resembled* order. I encourage you to give some thought to what you would like your days to look like, insofar as you can control them. The next twenty-one days will bear much more fruit if you do.

On a piece of paper, sketch out your day and break it into specific blocks of time. There are three steps to prioritizing your daily schedule effectively.

First, figure out which tasks *need* to be included in your day and which extras you *want* to include. Your priority list will be made up of both what you want to do and what you need to do.

Then, decide how much time you need to complete your daily tasks for each of your priorities, starting with the things you need to do. Many things on your list will take set blocks of time to complete, such as work, exercise, etc. However, many other priorities, such as reading a book or spending time with friends, will work on a sliding scale. You will want to factor those times into your schedule so that they do not overlap with other priorities.

Last, place each priority in its proper order. Each of your tasks will occupy a certain amount of time, but they also hold a certain rank as compared to the others. For example, your physical health is a high priority, but it is not as high of a priority as God. So if you were to schedule your morning routine, you'd want to block out a sufficient amount of time for prayer before starting a physical workout. Granted it will likely take longer to complete the workout than it will to pray, but the fact that you chose to honor God with the first fruits of your day shows that he is the higher priority. It isn't always about time; sometimes it is about rank.

Another example of how rank can beat out time is work versus family life. We dedicate many hours of our day to work and schooling, both necessary to ensure our family's survival and education. But these can tend to overshadow the hours of family quality time. Adults come home from work exhausted, and children return home from school lethargic, which requires a "recovery time" of sorts that will help us unwind. This makes our total amount of minutes with our family dwindle. If we grab our phones to occupy our recovery time as a family, we lose out on quality conversation, physical affection, and resting action for our minds and bodies. In the end, we spend more hours in our day working and recovering than we do with our own family members.

The best way to combat this process is to intentionally give each priority the time it deserves based on the time we have, and its rank.

Each person handles priorities differently, which is why I am not providing any single be-all and end-all schedule to imitate. Rather, I recommend that your daily routine reflect your priorities in both time and rank. If time spent in a lower priority must overshadow a higher one, may their ranks never be confused. For example, if you spend several hours a day at the gym, may those hours never become more *important* than the hours you have with your loved ones. Your daily schedule should account for this in some tangible way.

Limit Screen Time

There are two ways in which we use technology: (1) to efficiently consume and produce content and (2) to waste time.

There are also two realms in which we find ourselves using that technology: (1) at work or school and (2) for personal use.

In a perfect world we would use technology at work, school, and for personal use to efficiently consume and produce content. However, studies have shown that since the dawn of the smartphone we've spent much of our digital lives wasting time.

According a Pew Research Center Internet and Technology report, "Some 94% of smartphone owners carry their phone with them frequently and 82% say they never or rarely turn their phones off … with 59% reporting they use apps on their phones at least several times a day and 27% saying they use them 'continuously.'"[1]

This data, when coupled with the results from a study published on Forbes.com that claims 89 percent of people "admit wasting time at work every day,"[2] raises the question, what exactly are we doing with our devices?

---

[1] "Americans' Views on Mobile Etiquette, Chapter 1: Always on Connectivity," Pew Research Center, August 26, 2015, http://www.pewinternet.org/2015/08/26/chapter-1-always-on-connectivity/.
[2] "Wasting Time at Work: The Epidemic Continues," Forbes.com, July 31, 2015, https://www.forbes.com/sites/cherylsnappconner/2015/07/31/wasting-time-at-work-the-epidemic-continues/#2a13d3c61d94.

According to the mentioned Pew Research Center report, "About half of cellphone owners say that when they are in public, they use their phones for no particular reason — just for something to do — either frequently (18%) or occasionally (32%). By age, the differences are noteworthy: 76% of cell owners ages 18 to 29 use their phone at least occasionally in public for no particular reason, just for something to do."[3] In other words, half of the time that people are in public, at work, or studying, they are wasting time on their phones.

Your goal is to change that paradigm by limiting screen time to *only* efficient consumption and production for the next twenty-one days. I'll teach you how to do that as the retreat progresses.

Monitor Device Use

The final step toward detaching physically from the temptations of your phone is to download a monitoring app. Monitoring apps measure phone usage and report back to you how often you unlock your phone, what percentage of time you dedicate to which apps, and can even limit access to apps you choose.

When I first downloaded my monitoring app, I guessed that I was on my phone for thirty to forty-five minutes each day. Within the first six hours of downloading it, I had accumulated two and a half hours of phone use. I was flabbergasted at my underestimation.

We tend to rationalize destructive behaviors, especially when they are easy to hide from others. We carry our addictive behaviors with us every time we place our phone in our pockets. We think no one needs to know how often we act on our digital cravings, not even ourselves. We lie about our perceptions of our use of cellphones and underestimate their gravity, but a monitoring app places a mirror in front of us that shows the objective truth behind our addictive acts. They give us an objective number, and that number says a lot about who we are.

---

[3] "Americans' Views on Mobile Etiquette, Chapter 2: Phone Use in Public Area," August 26, 2015, http://www.pewinternet.org/2015/08/26/chapter-2-phone-use-in-public-areas/.

Visit detachedlife.com to see the latest and greatest monitoring apps for your phone. There you will find detailed instructions on how to download them (regardless of your make and model) and how to best use them during this time of retreat and beyond.

Sacrifice for Someone, or Something, Else

Our Catholic faith has a unique practice called "redemptive suffering." We believe that our sacrifices can affect the souls of those around us. We, like Jesus, can help strengthen those in need through the spiritual merits that our physical sufferings can achieve. Archbishop Fulton J. Sheen referred to this principle as a "spiritual blood transfusion" that brings others closer to their sanctification through our death to self.

During this twenty-one-day retreat, you will be sacrificing your addictive phone habits. This process will likely be difficult and uncomfortable, which is a form of suffering. To maximize the spiritual benefits of such a sacrifice, ask God to use the merits of your suffering to strengthen the soul of someone who is in desperate need of healing, whether spiritual or physical.

Saint Paul tells us, "Now I rejoice in my sufferings for your sake, and in my flesh I complete what is lacking in Christ's afflictions for the sake of his body, that is, the Church" (Col 1:24). Offer the next twenty-one days for the needs of your loved ones, the needs of the Church, or the needs of the souls in purgatory. Perhaps you have a friend or someone in particular who has a special need for spiritual assistance. Keep this intention close, and let it motivate you to persevere to the end. If you do, not only will you benefit from the process of detachment, but your sacrifices will also aid the one for whom you are offering your sufferings.

Today's tasks (creating a schedule, installing a monitoring app, and beginning to offer up your sacrifice) were designed to create a systematic foundation for your day. More importantly, they are steps on a pathway to holiness. Too often we live in a state of disorder because we try to move forward without a road map to follow. We do things willy-nilly based on the mood of the moment, and we end up frustrated that we never accomplish our goals. We become victims to fleeting passions and, as a result, become less passionate about the things that really matter in life.

If you take the time to order your life based on your priorities, you will find that life will feel more fulfilled. That's why this first day is focused on helping you establish a system that will set you up for success in detaching yourself from your tech. Think of it like the skeleton of your journey, a firm foundation on which everything else can have stability.

Tomorrow, we'll put some meat on those bones.

REFLECT

- For whom are you offering the sacrifices of this retreat?
- Why are you doing this for them?
- How many minutes of total time do you think you spend on your phone daily?
- What do you want to get out of this retreat?

PRAY

Father, you who know us so perfectly desire that we know you perfectly. Allow my heart and mind to be free from all that keeps me from knowing, loving, and serving you perfectly. Together with the Blessed Mother, all of the angels and saints, and those who struggled to overcome temptations of all kinds, bind me to your Son through the cross which I choose to bear as I make this retreat. May I endure this suffering with the help of your spiritual guidance. I offer these next few weeks for _____ .
Amen.

DAY 2

The Purge: Eliminating the Chaff

Yesterday you took the first steps toward detachment by creating a systematic schedule for your day. This system is the skeleton of your detached life in that it will keep everything else in its proper place. Today, fill that skeleton with everything else it needs to sustain a healthier, holier life.

When John the Baptist was baptizing people in the Jordan River, the Pharisees and Sadducees — the quintessential religious hypocrites of the time — came to be baptized. John had some pretty strong words for them: "When he saw many of the Pharisees and Sadducees coming for baptism, he said to them, 'You brood of vipers! Who warned you to flee from the wrath to come? Bear fruit that befits repentance'" (Mt 3:7–8).

The Pharisees and Sadducees had come because they were concerned with keeping face as the religious leaders of the people. John knew their empty intentions and so warned them to bear good fruit as a sign of their repentance. Good fruit can only be produced when all of the things that keep us away from holiness — the chaff — is discarded and only that which is good, holy, and pure — the wheat — remains.

John continued: "I baptize you with water for repentance, but he who is coming after me is mightier than I, whose sandals I am not worthy to carry; he will baptize you with the Holy Spirit and with fire. His winnowing fork is in his hand, and he will clear his threshing floor and gather his wheat into the granary, but the chaff he will burn with unquenchable fire" (Mt 3:11–12).

Our digital habits have a profound effect upon our souls. The things we access and spend time on become part of our identity. Our corporeal lives have become a reflection of our digital lives in so many ways that, at times, it is difficult to distinguish one from another. We spend more time interacting with friends and loved ones via text, social media, and phone calls than actual face-to-face interaction. Our phones have made it so fun and so efficient to share our lives and access information quickly that it is hard to discern what aspects of our device usage are wheat and what are chaff.

But deep down you know there is a difference.

Much of what we encounter on our devices is wheat. There are tremendous benefits to technology use on a daily basis. But, if you are taking this retreat seriously, it is likely that you feel there is more chaff in your digital life than good fruit. Let's work on getting rid of the chaff.

Detach from Each Device

If you are like most people, your cellphone is the primary culprit when it comes to screen addictions. It is the most compact, mobile, and fluid means to connect to the digital world. You are likely no more than ten feet away from it at any given moment throughout your day, and on the rare occasion you forget to bring it with you somewhere, you feel as if a part of you is missing.

If you are lucky enough to have other devices (let's call them "secondary" devices, such as a video-gaming system, laptop, tablet, or a piece of wearable tech such as a fitness band), then the chances of your success in this retreat are severely limited. You might be able to go without your phone for the entire duration, but the temptation to waste time using a different device will occur. When it does, you need to be strong enough to withstand it. Remember that this is a goal worth fighting for. Remember for whom you are making this sacrifice. Do it for them, for your own soul, for God.

Eliminate All Nonproductive Apps

There are two types of apps: (1) the ones that waste our time and (2) the ones that create more time for us to do the things we love.

We walk a very thin line when it comes to using apps for entertainment. Yes, we are supposed to enjoy ourselves, to relax and unwind through recreation, but doing so via an entertainment app (games, social media, online shopping, video streaming, and, yes, even reading) can become an addictive circle of constant activity. You might start by creating a post on social media and, while you wait for people to respond to it, you play a game. Once you beat the next level, you might open a reading app and start that new novel you just bought, but then, suddenly, you receive a push notification saying so-and-so left a comment on your post. You bounce back and forth like this until your mind is switching between several apps, overloading itself on a barrage of content instead of doing what you originally set out to do when you sat on the couch and took out your phone … to relax!

On the other hand, there are apps that can save time and energy. For example, you likely have a banking app that allows you to pay bills, transfer funds, and maybe even cash checks by taking a picture of them. This is a productive app. It takes away the burden of traveling to the bank to manage your money. This is the type of time-saving technology was properly designed to provide. It frees us from needless activity and creates time to do things that bring us true happiness. On top of that, it is not addictive by nature. I don't know of anyone who stays up until 3:00 a.m. because they are so engaged in their banking app.

For the next twenty days, eliminate every single app that wastes your time. Remember, this is a retreat, not an exodus. By deleting apps you are not committing to deleting entire accounts. You may decide to return to them after the retreat is over, which is fine and, for some people, may be necessary if your work requires you to use those apps regularly.

Start with entertainment apps. You don't need those. Your entertainment for the next twenty days (and hopefully for all time thereafter) will consist of many other things that we will discuss in future chapters.

Next, alert your social-media followers that you will be going on retreat. If you go straight to retreat mode without letting them know, some might think that something tragic happened to you, which will leave them with three weeks of angst and preoccupation before they realize you are fine. Don't be that friend. Give them the news by posting a status update saying something like the following: "I am fasting from Facebook for 21 days. Please pray for me and join me at detachedlife.com."

At detachedlife.com I've provided an image that can be used as your profile picture to remind yourself and your friends that you are on retreat. Download it, replace your current profile image, and then feel comfortable knowing you didn't leave your friends hanging while you basked in the glory of retreat time.

Finally, delete social-media apps. Social media can be used to efficiently market and campaign in the business world, but it can also take hours away from your day as you mindlessly scroll through friends' updates. You will find out how to properly schedule your social-media time in the chapters to come, but for the purpose of this retreat, eliminate the temptation by deleting them from your phone.

Put a Leash on Email

You are likely on the fence about deleting your email app, especially if it is necessary for work. Email is a particularly unique player in the game of behavior addiction. On one hand, we need it to effectively communicate with colleagues, professional and educational contacts, and family members. On the other hand, we need to regulate our use of email so that work doesn't overflow into personal or family time. Even then, there's always the temptation to be connected to work because you never know if leaving yourself out of the digital conversation will result in more work in the long run. In this case, it is not always possible to delete your email app.

However, for most of us, our email app can be relegated to a separate device — namely, our computers. That's why I recommend deleting your email app from your phone and regulating its use primarily through your computer. As a secondary way to control email activity, schedule the time you allot to reading, replying, writing, and sending emails on a daily basis. Make sure the time you dedicate to email is effective and reasonable. Once you've intentionally blocked off time, zealously remain faithful to that amount of time. When you're finished with email, promise yourself not to return to it until your scheduled time the next day. When you do this, you can live peacefully knowing you are not under the pressure to respond to incoming emails immediately; you are free to wait until the time you decide it is necessary.

Turn Off All Push Notifications for Necessary Apps

If you are absolutely certain that you need specific "necessary" apps for these twenty-one days, then do the next best thing and turn off push notifications. There is nothing worse for your spirit than random beeps that bear the burdens of anxiety and pressure. The instant they sound, you worry that if you don't stop everything you are doing to check your email, respond to a text, or "like" that person's comment on your social media post, your life will lose all meaning. Do yourself a favor and detach yourself from these perilous tones so that you, not your phone, can decide when to reply.

Keep Yourself Accountable

Aside from offering the sacrifices of this retreat for someone, it is highly recommended that you go forward with a partner as an added form of accountability. Granted, you are at liberty to complete the retreat by yourself, but your own willpower will help you only so far. You may need someone to hold you to your promises and help you make good on your goals.

That's why I recommend sharing the experience with someone close to you. It can be your spouse, a family member, a friend, or even a small group at your parish. If you find someone to complete this retreat with, the odds of success rise significantly.

Prepare to Retreat

All of the aforementioned suggestions are a means through which you are physically detaching from your phone. Once detached, you will find that you have all sorts of free time. With this free time will come several temptations. You'll want to grab your phone, check your email, scroll through your social media, etc.

Don't do that.

Instead, take those moments to read one chapter from this book each day. Allow your naturally philosophical mind to reflect and put into practice the wisdom I want to share with you in the following pages. This will allow you to escape mindlessly dawdling on your phone, and instead pursue excellence in your life through prayer, contemplation, meditation, and acts of virtue. In the end you'll discover your life is happier and holier for having persevered.

Congrats! You just finished day two.

REFLECT

- What are the hardest app(s) to delete from your phone? Why?

- What are your secondary devices and how often do you use them?

- What steps will you take to make sure your email activity is regulated?

- What types of "good fruit" do you hope will come out of this retreat?

PRAY

Dear Lord, the sound of your call to holiness has been quieted for some time now. May the sacrifice of my notifications illuminate my heart to a far greater degree than my screen, for in your light we see light. May your light shine in our souls and brighten the darkness that surrounds our attachment to worldly desires. Amen.

DAY 3
The Goal: True Happiness

God wants you to be happy. The problem is, you're not. Your life is filled with problems that need to be fixed, worries that keep you up at night, and responsibilities that call for your complete attention every waking hour of the day. Sometimes life becomes so overwhelming that you feel the need to escape.

So you do what millions of other people do at any given moment — you reach for your phone, tablet, or laptop, and you begin to scroll. Like a dive into a lake on a hot summer day, you eliminate the sights and sounds of the world and delve into the cool waters of the technological distraction.

I know. I've been there. I've escaped more than my fair share of times from the world in the same way. I've spent so many hours below the surface in this underwater retreat that I could have grown gills if I were biologically capable of doing so. The problem was, I'm not able to grow those gills, and as I spent more and more time in the abyss of technology, I began to drown.

The primary goal of this book is your happiness. Consider this retreat to be the life preserver that rescues you from the depths of technology overuse and guides you across the many rip currents of life toward a final destination of true, pure, and unfiltered joy. The journey will be long, difficult, and, at times, strenuous, but such is the way of living a truly Christian life. Imitating Christ demands we take up our cross and follow him regardless of the realities that exist in our lives. Good or bad, God beckons us to use these experiences to attain our potential for personal excellence.

You have been given a specific task to complete in this world, one that only you can complete. We are constantly changing — mind, soul, and body — in order to achieve this task. God grants us graces in every lesson we learn, every experience we have, and every relationship we make. Through these he forms us, always shaping us into a more perfect being. We become the best version of ourselves when we depart from this life and ultimately see God, for it is then that we achieve the fulfillment of all we have ever desired. This is what is meant by the potential of our personal excellence, that we will spend our lives seeking God and becoming more like him so that one day, according to Saint John, "we shall be like him, for we shall see him as he is" (1 Jn 3:2).

However, many things in our lives do, indeed, make us weaker and less able to fulfill the potential of our personal excellence. I believe technology overuse to be one of them.

Our Longing for Happiness

The world is obsessed with happiness. We seek it in our daily actions in the people we meet, the food we eat, the music we listen to, and even in the screens we use to distract us from the pressures of the world. Happiness is sought across genders, ages, social classes, cultures, continents. We are spiritually, mentally, psychologically, and physically built for it.

So the question we must begin with is, What is happiness? How can we properly define it?

The World's Definition of Happiness

According to the World Happiness Report, an annual index put out by the United Nations, happiness is measured by three subjective elements of well-being, which include:

1. Life Evaluation — a reflective assessment on a person's life or some aspect of it.
2. Affect — a person's feelings or emotional states, typically measured with reference to a particular point in time.
3. Eudaemonia — a sense of meaning and purpose in life, or a good psychological functioning.

The people who participate in this report are asked to answer the following question: "Please imagine a ladder, with steps numbered from zero at the bottom to ten at the top. The top of the ladder represents the best possible life for you and the bottom of the ladder represents the worst possible life for you. On which step of the ladder would you say you personally feel you stand at this time?"

The results are just what you might expect: richer countries fair better than poorer countries, and income, employment, education, family life, and both physical and mental health emerge as key factors when people determine which rung of the ladder their happiness is at.

While the factors evaluated are important and necessary in a person's well-being, safety, and ongoing growth, the metaphorical ladder can only reach so high. Even if one climbs up as high as rung number ten, he or she is only arriving at the sum of their physical and emotional feelings. True happiness goes beyond feeling or emotion. True joy is found in the soul.

The Catholic Definition of Happiness

According to Saint Thomas Aquinas, medieval scholar and Doctor of the Church, there are four levels of happiness, each of which can be mistaken for true, final happiness.

Natural Wealth

This level of happiness consists in possessing the basic needs that satisfy human survival as provided by nature. Food, drink, and shelter fit into this category, among other things. People who think they find happiness in this level believe that tasty food and drink and large elegant homes are the source of their joy. They fit as much on their plate as possible and stuff themselves to the point of gluttony in order to fall asleep in their king-sized beds, waking up only to do the same thing again the next day. Nature itself tells us that natural wealth can't be true joy, because after a certain point the body will refuse to take in another morsel and rebel through sickness and sloth. This is the shallowest form of happiness.

Artificial Wealth

If you lived before the implementation of money, you and your community would have traded resources such as cattle, land, cloth, etc. He who had the most resources was considered the wealthiest person. This person would gather wealth and, to a certain extent, you could say this person was happy; but, as it is true with money today, the feeling would be fleeting. Gathering artificial wealth ("artificial" in the sense of "manufactured or produced") is conditional. The more you have, the more difficult it becomes to sustain, because the future is always unknown.

For example, you might own a rather large plot of land along the coast of the Atlantic Ocean on which you have built several hotel chains and restaurants, a seemingly unstoppable flow of income. But if a natural disaster such as a hurricane hits the coast, or if the stock market crashes, all of that money you saved will be needed simply to rebuild. Artificial wealth creates a kind of psychologically deceptive happiness. It makes us believe that we are secure in a particular level of luxury. It produces a false security and a dependence on things, which ultimately leads us to yearn for something more, something greater than just things.

Interestingly, we see this idea of artificial wealth manifested every time a new device, especially if it is a phone, is unveiled to the public. People from all over the world stand in lines for days hoping they will be one of the first to shell over hundreds of dollars and unbox this new technology that will make their lives equally, if not more, distractible than the "older" version they currently hold in their pocket. This, and all forms of artificial wealth, do provide a certain degree of happiness, but it too is fleeting.

Honors and Glory

Honor and glory can be defined as the giving or receiving of accolades based upon acts made by people that are judged by society as worthy of praise. For example, when soldiers return home from war and receive a medal of honor, they are praised by the government for their acts of heroism. Or when musical artists win a Grammy, they are praised by the recording industry for their creativity in song.

When we seek happiness through honors, we inch closer to true happiness, but we inevitably fall short. When we recognize a particular good in another person, or when others recognize a particular good in us, we are doing something admirable. In fact, when you are the person being honored, this feeling of accomplishment can be life-changing and, depending on the good act, even world-changing.

The problem with happiness achieved through giving and receiving honor is twofold. First, sometimes the act that merits recognition was not done willfully, but on accident. People who receive honors merely for being in the right place at the right time, or simply for being popular, reasonably feel a sense of unworthiness for their "accolade" because they never meant to·do it in the first place. This is surely the exception to the norm, but nevertheless, it is brought up here to illustrate the defect in the argument for happiness through honors.

Second, the people who receive the honor live many other aspects of their lives as sinners. Granted this does not diminish the happiness they feel from their acts which are deserving of praise, but they still have room to grow in their potential for personal excellence. They still lack what they need to be truly fulfilled.

We all struggle with something — a vice, or several — that keeps us separated from God's love for us. While we might lead one specific aspect of our lives in a holy manner, there are other parts of our lives that we battle every second of our day to keep at bay. For example, the valedictorian of your high school may have been honored for his intelligence, but in the secret of his heart, maybe he struggled with the sin of pride, lust, or gluttony.

Temptation overcomes us and we willfully sin, adding an asterisk to any honor we receive. This is why many people refuse honors bestowed upon them, saying that they are undeserving of them because they are not 100 percent good. No one is. No one, that is, except God.

Honor and glory have a unique relation to technology addiction. Many of us feel a sense of validation whenever we post something on social media that receives several likes and shares. Writers strive for blogposts that reach millions through social media, video producers attempt to make every one of their creations go viral, users of any platform try to amass the most followers, and for what? To receive the fame and attention that come with honor and glory.

True Happiness

If you were to attain happiness in these first three levels of mentioned by Aquinas, you would surely record a perfect ten in the World Happiness Report. At the Life Evaluation level, people generally assesses their natural and artificial wealth as it pertains to their safety and well-being. At the Affect level, they assess their emotional state by how entertained they are, what educational level they have received, what type of limited power they have over others, etc. At the Eudaemonia level, people derive their psychological well-being by being honored for achieving success in whichever aspect of life they hold most dear — work, hobbies, relationships, etc. — which ultimately becomes their meaning in life, or what they think brings them happiness.

All of these, although objectively valuable and good in and of themselves, do not last. They can never be complete — we will always desire more natural wealth, artificial wealth, and honor or glory. True happiness, because it is God, is complete, which brings us to Aquinas's principal argument regarding the source of happiness — God himself.

The aforementioned forms of happiness are not altogether evil. They are only imperfect. This means that the pursuit of natural and artificial wealth, honor and glory does not always imply selfish acts of gluttony, greed, pride, or any of the other deadly sins. On the contrary, if pursued correctly, they can be catalysts to living a holy life. As mentioned previously, they are necessary rungs of a metaphorical ladder, but as Aquinas explained in his *Summa*, the only way we can achieve the goal of being truly happy is "by coming to know God and love him. … We call man's way of attaining his goal being happy." Therefore, regardless of whichever rung we are on, be it the height of economic success and mental stability, or the lows of poverty and clinical depression, we must take a giant leap toward the mystery of God if we desire to be truly and utterly happy.

Coming to know God is not an easy process, but it is a necessary one for anyone who desires to achieve true happiness. God is the very act of being and "in him all things hold together" (Col 1:17). Not a single cell nor a grain of sand, nor planet or galaxy would exist if it weren't for God's overflowing love. And it is in us, his most prized creations, that we are capable of becoming like him, for we were "created in his own image" (Gn 1:27). This is why the idea of our potential for personal excellence is so important; we long to become one with God; we desire more than all other forms of happiness to achieve our final end of eternal joy with him.

How do we get there? We *will* it.

We who exist within space and time are constantly drawn by the Holy Spirit who exists outside of space and time. To God, all time is a present moment. Every thought you have, every person you meet, every day the sun rises and sets upon the millions of creations he has made for you to experience is a means through which God draws you closer to his everlasting love. It is up to you to mindfully contemplate these miracles as you address his agenda and faithfully fulfill the mission he gives to you during your earthly life. You cannot come to these realizations until you have submitted your will to God's through a constant and consistent prayer life and a thirst for knowledge of the one omnipotent, omnipresent, and omniscient God of Christianity.

Technology use, and all other aspects of our lives, are only as good insofar as they lead us to this, our ultimate goal of knowing, loving, and serving God, and by striving to attain the full potential of our personal excellence through him. It goes deeper than merely downloading the Read the Bible in One Year app or saying your prayers before you go to bed. The totality of our lives must be an encounter with the Holy Spirit, who animates our souls and places within us the graces necessary to fulfill God's will over our own. The question you must ask yourself then is, Does the time you spend on your screen do this?

Today you've taken the first step to answering that question. In these remaining nineteen days, you will see the answer more clearly as I guide you through the method that will achieve this book's ultimate goal: your happiness, which will only be achieved through God's grace and sustained effort to achieve the fullest potential of your personal excellence.

Let's climb this ladder.

REFLECT

- Do you consider yourself a happy person? In what way?
- Do others perceive you as a happy person?
- Do those closest to you think you are happy?
- Does your screen use impact you positively, negatively, or both? How so?
- When are you the happiest?

PRAY

Merciful God, you are all that I desire in the land of the living.

In you I have placed all my hope and trust. Inebriate my soul so that my unending thirst for true joy may be quenched by your love for me. Fill me with your Holy Spirit so that I may become a joyful servant of your Son. Amen.

DAY 4
The Truth: Admitting Defeat

In 1997 I started my freshman year of high school. I went from an eighth-grade private school class of fourteen people to an incoming public school class of 550. The school had more than two thousand students and was more like a small college campus than a high school. In fact, the building itself was in its first year of operation and boasted eight separate pods, two for each level of academics, two gymnasiums, a colossal cafeteria, and, tucked into the back, a library surrounded by a wooded landscape that could be seen through the windows that surrounded its outside walls. I escaped to that library many times to "get away" from the busyness of such a highly populated school.

I was no scholar, and I hated reading books. The feeling of being surrounded by thousands of titles was intimidating, because I knew that I'd need to read many of them over the course of the next four years. Needless to say, reading did not excite me, and I often wondered why the library was my choice as a hiding place. One particular aspect of the library that drew me in was the dozen or so computers at an island in the middle of an open area. With only a username and a password, I could truly escape from the books, from the people, from the school itself, and be connected to a world beyond it all.

It wasn't long until I realized that most of my teachers didn't know how to use the internet. But a handful of other screen addicts, who frequently joined me in the library during any available moment, did. The books we had to read became online summaries that students from across the world had uploaded to make others' lives easier. The projects we had to complete became websites that we copied and from and pasted into a Word document to call our own. The physical friendships we lost out on were substituted with online friends who managed to sneak into their own school libraries and log on to messaging forums.

The library computers made life easier and more efficient. School was never an issue, because school was searchable, friends were findable, and access was limitless. As long as you could manage to get through each class, every moment thereafter would be yours. We seized each of these moments with the possibilities that technology offered.

This was my first real introduction to the "path of least resistance." This psychological term states that human beings are not wired to work hard, rather, we are more likely to do the bare minimum necessary for survival. With devices in our hands, we can lower that bare minimum even further. This was the path I followed to make my educational experiences more efficient, so that I could go about the rest of my day doing what I wanted to do. Ultimately, that efficiency created a cycle of technological vices that absorbed any free time I had.

According to attention expert Daniel Goleman, this is normal for human beings. For the vast majority of our existence, Homo sapiens have used the path of least resistance as a form of survival. Our brains have been conditioned to respond to our immediate environment in what Goleman calls a "bottom-up" manner. He writes, "The bottom-up system multitasks, scanning a profusion of inputs in parallel, including features of our surroundings that have not yet come into full focus; it analyzes what's in our perceptual field before letting us know what it selects as relevant for us."[4] Hence, our ancestors' constant awareness of the stimuli for survival was passed on to us, and our

---

[4] Daniel Goleman, *Focus: The Hidden Driver of Excellence* (New York: Harper, 2013), 26.

minds seek the quick fix for survival, entertainment, and pleasure before everything else.

Throughout the course of human history, however, our immediate needs became dependable. We established communities, planted crops, and developed efficient ways to ensure our survival, protection, and flourishing. We no longer had to keep our guard up against the threat of leaping tigers or lunging snakes. At this point, humans became free to think beyond their own basic needs. This was when we developed "top-down" brain patterns, which allowed our brains to explore things such as creativity, ingenuity, and religion.

Goleman continues: "Top-down wiring adds talents like self-awareness and reflection, deliberation, and planning to our mind's repertoire. Intentional, top-down focus offers the mind a lever to manage our brain. As we shift our attention from one task, plan, sensation or the like to another, the related brain circuitry lights up. Bring to mind a happy memory of dancing and the neurons for joy and movement spring to life. Recall the funeral of a loved one and the circuitry for sadness activates. Mentally rehearse a golf stroke and the axons and dendrites that orchestrate those moves wire together a bit more strongly."[5]

It seems logical to believe that in today's technologically advanced world we have all of our immediate survival needs fulfilled, leaving us with most of the day to focus, ponder, and bask in the tasks of top-down thought. But this is rarely the case. In fact, the opposite is true: We are more distracted than ever with many tasks, and phones have become a secondary distraction that ensures that our minds are constantly working at the bottom-up level. While we have children to raise, we are on the couch jonesing for "likes" on social media. While our dinner burns in the oven, we are oblivious as long as we get the high score in our games. When it is time for us to meditate on the things of God, we check our email so that we can perform better at work.

---

[5] Ibid., 27.

When I was in high school, I became lethargic in my abilities to think and act due to my technology-induced, bottom-up thinking. When I had to memorize certain facts for tests, but I could not use a computer, my ability to retain these bits of information was stifled by habitual dependence on the computer's search engine. I found myself unable to focus on things I formerly could focus on with ease — interpreting a poem, looking at art, memorizing lyrics from songs. Even face-to-face conversation with my peers became difficult to bear. When I found myself speaking with others, I couldn't even look them in the eye because I was so preoccupied with how I could get through the conversation while still looking attentive so as not to be rude. I was always looking for a polite way to exit conversations and be on my way, as if I was in a hurry to move on to the next daily task as quickly as I could click from link to link on the screens. In short, my daily life become a microcosm of my technological habits.

Technology, when coupled with the path of least resistance, weakens the mind and cripples the will. It is the answer to our lazy prayers. It multiplies the possibilities to commit the sins that we struggle most to avoid, each of which is easily identified by a simple connection that we rarely ever make because it pains us to admit that we blindly follow the vices that dominate each realm of our digital lives. These are called "hooks," and they are devilishly designed to ensure that we become addicted to them. They are designed to ensure that we are constantly and consistently connected to using them, so that the developers can capitalize on our curiosity in the form of advertising, downloads, and, ultimately, profits. They do this by creating a hook specific to your natural curiosity and sense of bottom-up need. Unfortunately, this sense of need is grounded in the vices that tempt us the most. Each hook has within itself a specific temptation that corresponds to one of the seven deadly sins:

- Lust drives the porn industry.
- Gluttony dwells in the online shopping community.

- Greed surrounds the online gambling community.
- Sloth inhabits the gaming community.
- Wrath occupies the comment boxes in the blogging community.
- Envy perches atop the social-media community.
- Pride abides in the email community.

These hooks, of course, are not the only things that lead us to behavioral addictions, but they are gateways into other activities that feed our distractibility. Technological vice also exists in streaming videos, exercise monitoring, video chatting, etc. These hooks became normalized behavior addictions. Society has deemed technology addiction acceptable, to the point that everywhere you go today you will likely see men and women, boys and girls of all ages staring at a screen, attempting to escape from the world, only to be attached to the world within.

The reality of the social normalization of technology addiction is reaching the level of critical emergency. According to recent statistics: 46 percent of people say they couldn't bear to live without their smartphones; the average adult spends an average of two hours and forty-eight minutes on their phone per day, totaling roughly twenty hours per week viewing just that one screen, which is the equivalent of working a part-time job; there are more than 280 million smartphone addicts, which, if put together, would be the fourth most populous country in the world.[6]

We are addicted to our devices, and this truth has serious, spiritual ramifications. Technology has made it easier than ever for the devil to manifest his temptations into our lives. It works because we defer to that which is easy and distractible as opposed to that which is difficult and worthwhile. Together technology and the path of least resistance widen the road that leads to your soul's destruction, "and those who enter by it are many" (Mt 7:13).

To see how you fare regarding your level of technology ad-

---

6 Adam Alter, *Irresistible: The Rise of Addictive Technology and the Business of Keeping Us Hooked* (New York: Penguin Press, 2017).

diction, answer the following questions with complete honesty.

Select the response that best represents the frequency of each behavior listed using the scale below:

0 = Not applicable
1 = Rarely
2 = Occasionally
3 = Frequently
4 = Often
5 = Always

How often do you find that you stay online longer than you intended?

How often do others in your life complain to you about the amount of time you spend online?

How often do you check your email before something else that you need to do?

How often do you lose sleep because of late night log-ins?

How often do you find yourself saying "just a few minutes" when online?

If you scored 0–7, you show no signs of internet addiction. A score of 8–12 suggests mild internet addiction. A score of 13–20 indicates moderate internet addiction, which means you have "occasional or frequent problems" in life due to your relationship with technology. If you scored between 21–25, you likely have severe internet addiction, which is causing "significant problems" in your life and mental capabilities.[7]

It is time to recognize reality and admit defeat. We are addicted to our screens and need to do an immediate about-face in

---

[7] Ibid.

the way we use technology. However, whatever your level of addiction is, all is not lost. We can redirect the GPS of our souls by using our screens to build up virtue as we travel on the straight and narrow path to a happier, holier life.

REFLECT

- Do you consider yourself addicted to your phone? Were you surprised by the quiz results?
- What types of real-world realities have you substituted for digital versions — for example, online interaction with friends versus face-to-face meetings, purchasing items online instead of going to the store, etc.?
- What is your root "hook" when it comes to screen use?
- How often are you able to spend time in top-down thought? When you have the time, do you choose to do so?
- How do you think God is calling you to use technology in your daily life?

PRAY

Almighty God, I come to you a sinner. Have mercy on me. I desire with my entire being to be united with you in love. Please help me untie the knots that have kept my soul bound to worldly things. Make all of my desires pure, and please, if it be your will, provide for me the graces to overcome my earthly passions. I am yours. Amen.

DAY 5

The Enemy: Distraction

In *The Screwtape Letters*, by C. S. Lewis, a senior demon named Screwtape trains his nephew, a junior tempter named Wormwood, through a series of letters that explain how to lead a human soul away from God and toward eternal hellfire. Screwtape often refers to God as "the Enemy" in his letters, and at one point urges Wormwood not to get too overzealous in tempting his human because doing so might cause the subject to realize the rashness of his immoral decisions and thus contemplate the mercy of the Enemy:

> As this condition becomes more fully established, you will be gradually freed from the tiresome business of providing Pleasures as temptations. As the uneasiness and his reluctance to face it cut him off more and more from all real happiness, and as habit renders the pleasures of vanity and excitement and flippancy at once less pleasant and harder to forgo (for that is what habit fortunately does to a pleasure) you will find that anything or nothing is sufficient to attract his wandering attention. You no longer need a good book, which he really likes, to keep him from his prayers or his work or his sleep; a column of advertisements in yesterday's paper will do. You can make him waste his time not only in conversation he enjoys with

people whom he likes, but in conversations with those he cares nothing about on subjects that bore him. You can make him do nothing at all for long periods. You can keep him up late at night, not roistering, but staring at a dead fire in a cold room. All the healthy and outgoing activities which we want him to avoid can be inhibited and nothing given in return, so that at last he may say, as one of my own patients said on his arrival down here, 'I now see that I spent most of my life in doing neither what I ought nor what I liked.' ...

Indeed the safest road to hell is the gradual one — the gentle slope, soft underfoot, without sudden turnings, without milestones, without signposts.[8]

Our "Enemy," of course, is not God, but rather Satan, and his primary weapon is not an atomic bomb of temptations to commit mortal sins such as murder or robbing banks. Rather, his fundamental mode of destruction is distraction: a compact weapon that deals out constant stealth blows to divide the soul from its Creator.

We first see the devil dividing humanity from God in the Book of Genesis when he tempts Adam and Eve into eating the fruit from the tree of knowledge of good and evil. He comes to them as a serpent, described as "more subtle than any other wild creature" (3:1). First he asked Eve whether or not she could eat of all of the trees in the Garden of Eden. He did this to slowly draw her into desiring, under her own initiative, disobedience toward the God who loved her. As the story unfolds, Eve recoils from the devil at first, but begins to let her passions dominate her will.

Then the devil says, "God knows that when you eat of it your eyes will be opened, and you will be like God, knowing good and evil" (v. 5). The Genesis text continues, "So when the woman saw that the tree was good for food, and that it was a delight to the eyes, and that the tree was to be desired to make one wise, she took of its fruit and ate; and she also gave some to her husband, and he ate" (v. 6).

[8] C. S. Lewis, *The Screwtape Letters* (repr., New York: HarperOne, 2015), Letter 12.

Eve's motivation went from following God's rules, which were oriented toward an unimaginable future happiness, to following her own passion to satisfy her "delight" for wisdom. The devil subtly put two good things in front of Eve to choose between: one that had divine light as its end, and another that led to darkness. Eve chose the latter, and in her distracted state she lost sight of what she truly desired — namely, coexistence with God and the total joy that comes with it.

What is our primary reason for having a device that has the potential of providing us with every piece of knowledge the world has ever known? The answer should be simple: We desire wisdom, and there, in your pocket, is access to unlimited resources to satiate, organize, encourage, and achieve the ends of that desire with mind-blowing efficiency. If this were the primary way we used technology, we'd be like Adam and Eve before the Fall, lavishing in the natural paradise that our digital tools have the potential to create. But, to the contrary, the devil has convinced us that our screens are not tools but companions, little Screwtapes and Wormwoods constantly distracting us from the God-given wisdom we seek.

The following scenario probably sounds familiar: You are walking down the street to get to your next venue and you are curious to know what time it is so that you won't arrive late. You reach for your phone to check the clock and see that you have plenty of time before you need to be there, so you stop, unlock your screen and check your calendar to make sure you have the right time for the appointment. You then check your email to see if anyone has contacted you about other work you have been delaying. Then, after finishing these "required" tasks, you take a break to check your social media feed. You scroll and scroll until you recognize posts from the last time you logged on. Then, to relax, you start playing a game. Before you know it, you have only a couple of minutes to get to your destination, but you forgot that you had to go to the bathroom. You call ahead to say you'll be a little late. As you enter the building, you close the bathroom door and unlock your screen again to start the whole process over again, this time with a mind that switches from "What do I need to do here again?" to "I better hurry up!"

Your primary motivation in using the phone as a tool was to check the time, but you became distracted. As a result, you arrived late, had to rush to the bathroom, and lost your full focus on the task you originally set out to do.

This series of events is not uncommon. In fact many people go through it several times a day. It is no wonder that the word demon comes from the Greek word *daimon*, "to divide." Such was the will of Uncle Screwtape for his nephew: to distract with subtle sinfulness. It is also no small wonder that the word device has a similar root word, derived from the Latin *dividere*, which means both "to desire" and "to divide."

The truth of the matter is that we, like Adam and Eve before us, desire wisdom, but more often than not we attain a false wisdom when we reach for our phones. We think we are unlocking our minds when we enter our password-protected digital worlds, but what we are really unlocking is a Pandora's box of limitless temptations. This provides the devil and his demons with enough force to divide us further away from God through our distracted minds. Instead of using technology to advance in knowledge of God and to contemplate his wisdom, we settle for mindless scrolling on social media and high-point scores on the latest gaming fad. As a result, we ignore God's constant call to holiness and opt for something of much lesser value — the very devices that divide us from him.

Uncle Screwtape would be very proud.

REFLECT

- From what do you desire to be distracted?
- Have you ever had to decide between two good things in your life? How did you make your decision?
- Have you ever turned on your phone with the intent to accomplish one task, but found yourself forgetting about it

completely after distracting yourself with other, nonessential tasks?

- How often do your pray to your guardian angel for guidance against the temptations of the devil?

PRAY

Holy Father, you gather everything in existence to yourself. Even the devil must acknowledge that, without you, he could not exist. May I recognize this truth in my heart at every moment of my day, especially when tempted to distract myself from completing all that you have asked me to do. Amen.

DAY 6

The Miracle: You Are an Artistic Masterpiece

My apologies, but I fear the past few chapters have been a bit doom and gloom. There is, however, a fantastic flip side to all of that: God has placed in our nature an inexpressible joy for those who are able to overcome the obstacles of worldly distraction.

Human beings are, by our nature, miracles. Saint Peter tells us, "His divine power has granted to us all things that pertain to life and godliness, through the knowledge of him who called us to his own glory and excellence, by which he has granted to us his precious and very great promises, that through these you may escape from the corruption that is in the world because of passion, and become partakers of the divine nature" (2 Pt 1:3–4). The problem is that we aren't quite sure just how to arrive at this sharing of divine nature because our evil desires are so strong. Our human reasoning allows us to go only so far. It is a paradox that we, who are destined to live with God for eternity and to be like him in nature, are only able to understand so little of his marvelous ways.

We thus contemplate along with the psalmist when he says:

For you formed my inward parts,
you knitted me together in my mother's womb.

I praise you, for I am wondrously made.
Wonderful are your works!
You know me right well;
my frame was not hidden from you,
When I was being made in secret,
intricately wrought in the depths of the earth.
Your eyes beheld my unformed substance;
in your book were written, every one of them,
the days that were formed for me,
when as yet there was none of them.
How precious to me are your thoughts, O God!
How vast is the sum of them!
If I would count them, they are more than the sand.
When I awake, I am still with you. (Ps 139:13–18)

Our eternal soul thus drives us toward truth. In other words, we hold within us a potential for excellence that can only be fulfilled and perfected by God. He who formed us teaches us how to live our lives in the person of his Son, Jesus Christ, who stands before us as the perfect example of holiness. In Jesus we see the human and divine nature coexisting for eternity, and it is through him that we learn to "be perfect, as your heavenly Father is perfect" (Mt 5:48) by assenting to the state of partakers in his divine nature. All that we need to do is hunger for holiness, and then "God will satisfy our longing, good measure, and flowing over."[9]

So how do we do that? How does one "hunger" for holiness? Truthfully, we all do this naturally because we all philosophize. We ask ourselves the deep questions about life such as, "Why am I here?" and "What's my purpose in life?" As mentioned previously, we ask these questions primarily because they concern our happiness. We want to know the answers because we know that when we find them, we'll lead a more fulfilled life — one with purpose, meaning, and joy.

---

[9] Divine Office Psalter, Week 2, Evening Prayer Antiphon curing Ordinary Time.

We answer these questions by using our reason. God has given us a gift — intellect — that separates us from all other forms of life. We are not rocks that merely exist, nor plants or animals that live without a rational soul. Rather, we are a composite of body and soul that not only exists, but lives, moves, feels, reasons, and thinks. In short, the human person is God's masterpiece, gifted with capabilities that begin and end in an all-powerful, all-knowing, and all-good God. In his love, we, and everything else, exist.

Our reason is what makes us special. It drives us. It manifests itself in every one of our actions. It not only forces an awareness upon us regarding the effects of these actions, but also lays out a plan for happiness. When you were a kid, and you broke the side window on accident, your reason told you one of two things: you could fess up and tell your parents that you did it, or you could lie by not saying anything or by telling them someone else did it. Your reason told you to pick the one that would likely get you in the least trouble. Or, if you had high moral standards (and bravery), you knew the right decision was to tell the truth; because otherwise the guilt would have driven you crazy in the long run.

Today reason is telling you that your use of technology is keeping you from true happiness. As a rational being, you know that there is more to life than the countless hours you have spent looking at a screen with nothing to show for it besides a high score in the game you just downloaded or the seven "likes" you received on the picture you took of your lunch. Your reason is telling you there is something more to explore, something that is worth more than the expensive phone you carry and the monthly plan your provider charges you to be almost constantly distracted.

You are a human being. You are a miracle. You are destined for excellence in this life and greatness in the next. Jesus himself said, "Truly, truly, I say to you, he who believes in me will also do the works that I do; and greater works than these he will do" (Jn 14:12). Your screen can be a potent tool in making this happen.

But right now, as you are seeking answers on this retreat,

it is holding you back from the perfection you desire. It causes you to pursue life's ultimate questions less. It is a finite thing that does not fulfill the power of your intellect. It entertains you with ignorance and scatters your attention, making it almost impossible for your brain to focus on a single deep thought. It keeps you far away from your life goals and lessens your desire to achieve them.

In short, your screen is the anti-you at this point. But it doesn't have to be that way.

REFLECT

- In what ways is your phone the anti-you?
- What potential effects does your reason have on your soul?
- The will is a power of the soul that can overcome all of our passions, both positive and negative. How do you overcome your negative passions?

PRAY

My Lord, you created me for greatness. You have given me a purpose, one that is unique and clear if only I would give you all of my faith. Guide me toward that clarity where my will is united to yours so that each of my actions will bring glory to your name. Amen.

DAY 7

The Foundation of Holiness: Your Priorities

Your days are numbered.

From the moment you were conceived in your mother's womb, you've existed within space. As a result, you've had to abide by the rules of physics and time. You haven't conquered gravity and flown like Superman, nor have you discovered Neverland and remained young forever like Peter Pan. Your time and physical capabilities are limited, and that's what makes life interesting.

There is an urgency to life when we realize that we are only given so many days to live, so many breaths to breathe. For many people this realization doesn't hit them until they reach their forties or fifties. They spend their entire lives establishing careers, families, and security, and they forget about the things in life that are really important. In pursuit of money and power, they sacrifice close relationships only to replace them with work-related ones, and often ultimately lose themselves to gain economic stability. Many people experience a midlife crisis because they realize they have spent so much time merely passing through life that they have forgotten to actually live it.

Today screens have contributed to this distraction, leading us away from the realization that our time on earth is limited. Historically, when alone with our thoughts after a long day, we would prioritize our desires and needs, making mental lists of what we were able to accomplish that day and what we could do to efficiently complete tomorrow's tasks. From there we would begin to philosophize on what goals could be dreamed up in order to better ourselves in the weeks, years, and decades to come. We then began to map out ways to achieve those goals, devising how to learn the skills necessary to attain our personal excellence. In short, we would prioritize our lives during those moments of deep thought, moments which today's screens rob us of every time we take our phones with us as we tuck ourselves into bed each night.

Granted, not all our failures can be chalked up to screen usage — ignorance, poor choices, even bad luck can be heavy hitters when it comes to our understanding of what matters most. However, I think we can all agree that with a limited amount of days to live our lives, screens are taking up a huge chunk of time that can be better used in other, more important aspects of life.

What are your priorities? Every person in the world has a unique way in which they approach their priority lists. Each individual has the free will to choose what they value most. The key factor that all our activities have in common is time. How much time you dedicate to specific tasks is directly related to how high they are on your priority list.

Not all tasks are equal, however. The desire to do certain tasks is determined by several factors, including survival, a sense of security, the enjoyment received from doing them, and a sense of accomplishment or belonging experienced because of them. The act of work, for example, might not be enjoyable for some, but it is necessary to dedicate forty hours per week to it because it provides financial security in the form of income and other benefits. This act, because it takes such a large chunk of time and is vital for survival, would naturally be high on your priority list.

On the other hand, playing basketball on Tuesday nights for two hours may fit into your priority list, too, because it provides you with exercise, friendships, and enjoyment. While these things might seem more important to you than financial security, in actuality, they aren't. Why? Because you are willing and able to dedicate more time to work than shooting hoops. You wouldn't think of quitting your job in order to dedicate forty hours each week to play hoops with your buddies. It would be both irresponsible and unwise to sacrifice your livelihood for your enjoyment.

Yet, that's exactly what we do when we reach for our screens — we sacrifice things that should be highest on our priority list for something much lower. We leave our dinners to burn in the oven, we forget to sign our kids up for swimming lessons, or we stay up later than we should, cramming for that history final all because we stayed up late binge watching the latest television series. In essence, we forget what matters most because we are unwilling to give technology precisely the level of priority it deserves, and no higher.

The question then is, how do we get our priorities in order? What actually is most important in life? The answer can be found in the simplicity of the prayer Christ taught us — the Lord's Prayer, also known as the Our Father.

According to Saint Thomas Aquinas, "In the Lord's Prayer not only do we ask for all that we may rightly desire, but also in the order wherein we ought to desire them, so that this prayer not only teaches us to ask, but also directs all our affections."[10] Since the fall of Adam and Eve, we have been cursed with an incessant desire to do what is contrary to our own happiness. Saint Paul reiterates this sentiment: "I do not understand my own actions. For I do not do what I want, but I do the very thing I hate" (Rom 7:15). When we pray the Lord's Prayer, we're essentially asking God to help us get our priorities in the correct order so that we can do the things that will bring us true joy.

Over the next several chapters let's take a look at the Lord's Prayer and break it down line by line to discover what things should make it to our priority list and what weight we should give to each of them.

---

[10] Thomas Aquinas, *Summa Theologica*, I-II, Q. 83, A. 9.

Our Father, who art in heaven, hallowed be thy name.

The prayer begins with the possessive pronoun "our." It doesn't start with "my" or "your" for a reason — God is the Creator of all life, and therefore we have a responsibility to worship him as a community. More often than not we tend to keep God for ourselves, embedded in a relationship with him that is only acted upon when we are in dire need. It isn't until life gets difficult that we turn our heads to the heavens and ask for help. The truth is that, while we must lift our eyes to heaven every day whether life is good or bad, we must also look left and right and recognize the people around us in order to build up within one another that spiritual zeal of faith. We are in this life together, and our Father in heaven wants us operating as one body with many parts (see 1 Cor 12:12–27) with God himself as the head and we, his children, making up the rest of his physical and spiritual body.

We operate as one family so that we may be made worthy of the promises of Christ and achieve faith's goal: complete unity with God who art in heaven. Saint Paul tells us, "For our knowledge is imperfect and our prophecy is imperfect; but when the perfect comes, the imperfect will pass away" (1 Cor 13:9–10). This means that, while on earth, we are hidden in the darkness of spiritual ignorance so that we can pursue true knowledge with an honest heart. When our faith is united with our zeal for knowledge, we come that much closer to our heavenly homeland, where we will no longer see God "in a mirror dimly," but "face to face" (1 Cor 13:12).

We pursue this knowledge by honoring God, making him the primary source of our hope and joy. We do this by ensuring that his name is hallowed. The word "hallow" means to honor as holy. God is the holiest being in existence, and he loves us enough to allow us to exist as creatures made in his image and likeness. Here's the thing — none of us is worthy of any of his love. We are sinners and deserve much worse than what we are given. Quite literally, we deserve hellfire, pain, and suffering because of our sinful ways. But God gives us chance after chance, new day after new day, to live better, holier lives. As such, it seems only logical that we should do everything within our power to love him in return.

We are indebted to his mercy, and if we truly understand this, we become his slaves, recognizing that we owe all we are to him. We must be at his beck and call, ready to carry out his service at any given time, because in doing his will we honor him as holy and thus become more like him. It is the paradox of Christianity that we who humble ourselves to the point of becoming God's slaves become truly free. "For he who was called in the Lord as a slave is a freedman of the Lord" (1 Cor 7:22). And in this slavery, and freedom, we find happiness.

The first three priorities the Lord gives us in the Lord's Prayer are:

1. Recognize that we approach God as a community of believers.
2. Make getting to heaven your ultimate goal.
3. Do everything within your power to honor God.

REFLECT

- How do you keep God first in your life?
- What is your prayer life like?
- What is your favorite way to pray?
- Would others consider you a "man or woman of God"?

PRAY

O my God, I am yours. I come to you humbly as your servant and thank you for all you have done in my life. I love you and submit myself to your will. Give me the courage and fortitude to follow your commands. Amen.

DAY 8

Thy Kingdom Come: Heaven on Earth

Thy kingdom come; thy will be done on earth as it is in heaven.

Since you own a device, you probably know the "I gotta have it" syndrome. Whether for survival or entertainment purposes, we view many things as items we "gotta have." When the newest device goes on the market, throngs of people stand in line for days in order to be the first ones to connect it to their network. As time goes by, the thing they were once so excited about is replaced by the next thing that they just "gotta have."

While some of these things are great resources and may have unmatched potential to make our lives easier and more efficient, the fact of the matter is that none of them are truly necessary. We pay hundreds, even thousands, of dollars to satisfy our desires because we believe these things will fulfill us. We think they will make us more connected, more knowledgeable, and better able to live our lives to the fullest.

I have some news for you: In heaven, there is no Wi-Fi. You will not be fulfilled by the things of this world. You will only be fulfilled by love.

God is an overflowing torrent of love. His love is so abundant that it overflows from his kingdom in heaven into our existence. When we pray "thy kingdom come," we recognize this overlap of his love in our lives. In fact, we aren't just recognizing it, we are welcoming it, daring him to pour it all over us!

Asking God to bring his kingdom to us is dangerous — it will inevitably lead to changes in our thoughts, feelings, and desires. We transform into something we are not, something much greater, much holier than we currently are — we become Christ. Saint Paul reminds us that when we ask God's kingdom to come, we "have been crucified with Christ; it is no longer I who live, but Christ who lives in me; and the life I now live in the flesh I live by faith in the Son of God, who loved me and gave himself for me" (Gal 2:20).

When this happens, we transform from an "I gotta have it" person to an "I gotta have him" person. As a result, we are given more connectivity, more knowledge, and more life than any device could ever offer. When God takes over your soul, he connects you to his Wi-Fi, and your will becomes synced with his. Your mind then begins to think about the things of God before you even act. It is in this mindset that you become one with Jesus, who in return shows you how to "seek first his kingdom and his righteousness, and all these things shall be yours as well" (Mt 6:33). When we are connected to God's Wi-Fi, we receive the fullness that we are seeking when we wait in line for the latest shiny new device.

God's Wi-Fi is powered by love, and the most effective way to connect to it is to love those whom God has placed in your life. He put you into your family for a reason. He may have blessed you (or will bless you in the future) with a partner and children because of an overflowing torrent of his love. He may have given you the grace to remain single in order to minister to his people as a layman, laywoman, religious brother or sister, or a priest. Focusing on the salvation of those whom you have been called to serve is your second highest priority after attaining your own.

It isn't selfish to put your own salvation over others. On the contrary, if you truly do desire salvation, you attend to others' needs and recognize them as more important than your own. Christians maintain a unique paradox in that the only way of attaining our goal of holiness is by becoming less concerned with ourselves and more concerned with the needs of others. When we do this correctly, we do God's will "on earth as it is in heaven." In other words, God's love manifests itself in our words and actions, and we become a precursor of the eternal perfection we hope for.

The second set of priorities given to us in the Lord's Prayer are:

4.   Allow God's love to overlap into your life.
5.   Act upon that love so others can attain salvation, too.

REFLECT

- Who are the people God has placed in your life to serve?
- Do you consider yourself to be a good servant to others?
- When have you noticed God's kingdom on earth?
- What steps do you plan on taking to advance God's kingdom on earth from this moment on?

PRAY

God, you are all that is and ever will be. You have sent me into this world to help heal it. To make it easier, you gave me those who love me to teach me how to grow in holiness. May I continue that mission by giving to others as you have given to me. May I be open to the needs of others and humble enough to meet those needs as well as I am able. Amen.

DAY 9
Our Daily Bread: Your Place in the Story of Salvation

Give us this day our daily bread; and forgive us our trespasses as we forgive those who trespass against us.

Baking bread is an art form. In order for it to come out perfect, you need to gather the ingredients, follow the recipe, and make sure it bakes at the right temperature. It is a peculiar process, because we are motivated to bake to fulfill our hunger. But if we bake when we're hungry we might make mistakes — lose our focus, burn the crust, or add too much yeast. When we make these mistakes, we pay for it, as our stomachs remind us of our errors. After failed attempts, we pick up the baking utensils and try again, because we cannot leave our hunger unsatisfied. We need material sustenance to survive. Hence, being a baker or a cook is an art form that requires hunger, focus, and balance.

When we ask God to give us our daily bread, we are asking him, the Master Baker, to teach us how to properly order our lives so we not only survive the daily grind that sustains us but thrive in the act of completing his will in our lives. We do this through work.

The term "work" refers to anything done because you either need or would like to see a change in the world around you. It involves your personal life as well as your professional life. Teaching my children their multiplication tables is just as much a part of my work as is writing this book or removing weeds from my garden. From the moment we wake up, we recognize a lack of beauty, order, or truth in the world, and we look within our souls to discover we have the means to change it, to bring about the beauty, order, and truth we seek. So we make to-do lists, both at our workplaces and at home, in order to bring about the changes needed or desired.

Professional work is a marvelous thing, because it provides us with a certain degree of satisfaction, a paycheck, and security. This type of work is your nine-to-five that pays the bills and makes sure there is food in the fridge when you get home every evening. For some, professional work provides immense satisfaction; for others, not so much. Either way, this work is necessary because it not only sustains us physically but also teaches us about a work ethic and character. Saint Paul reminds us of its importance: "If any one will not work, let him not eat. For we hear that some of you are walking in idleness, mere busybodies, not doing any work. Now such persons we command and exhort in the Lord Jesus Christ to do their work in quietness and to earn their own living" (2 Thes 3:10–12).

Personal work, on the other hand, is separated into two categories — responsibilities and passions.

Responsibilities refer to household duties and physical maintenance such as cleaning the bathroom and brushing your teeth. Granted, some of these tasks have higher priorities than others — you wouldn't spend three hours cleaning the storage unit if your kitchen, bathroom, and sleeping quarters were a disaster, especially if you were expecting company. You'd also want to take a shower once all that work was complete as a service to your visitors. Maintaining a healthy household and body requires that you place each of these responsibilities at the forefront of your priority list and execute them with consistency and right judgment; otherwise your household might explode, or you might become terribly ill.

The other form of personal work is the one we all love — our passion. Your passion is the thing that makes you want to get out of bed every morning. It is the driving force in your life, the activity you would gladly do twenty-four hours a day, seven days a week if you didn't have to complete other work-life responsibilities. God graces us with these passions and motivations. The secular world calls this a "muse" — a spark of interest, a flair of motivation to do something that will benefit ourselves and, ultimately, the world. For some, this might be writing a novel; for others, it might be training to run a marathon. Regardless of who you are or what you are internally inspired to do or create, this inspiration to do something good, true, and beautiful is from God. He provides us with the talent, motivation, and time to fulfill our passions. When we successfully complete them, we honor God and fulfill his will for his benefit, our benefit, and the benefit of others. It is a win-win-win situation.

The problem, however, is that we oftentimes lose because we are prone to prioritizing our work incorrectly. Some people choose to spend more time in the office than at home with their children. Others dedicate more time to a side business than with their spouses. Still others stay up late binge watching streamed movies and wake up early the next morning unable to focus at school. We take on too much, and in doing so we ignore the things that matter most — the people whom we journey with in this life.

This is why Jesus taught us to pray not only for our daily bread, but for the ability to forgive others in the same way he forgives us, even when our work-life balance places him at the bottom of our priorities. Our imperfections drive him crazy in the same way others' imperfections drive us crazy, if not more. But we must respond the way God responds, with an outpouring of love to those who surround us at work, at home, and especially to ourselves.

As Saint Paul so eloquently put it: "Love is patient and

kind; love is not jealous or boastful; it is not arrogant or rude. Love does not insist on its own way; it is not irritable or resentful; it does not rejoice at wrong, but rejoices in the right. Love bears all things, believes all things, hopes all things, endures all things" (1 Cor 13:4–7).

To seek forgiveness from God is to place him at the forefront of our lives. To forgive others when they put us at the bottom of their priority list, or trespass against us in any other way, is the first step in making them rise to the top of our priority lists. Perhaps when they are there, they will have the same mercy on us when we fail to maintain our priorities correctly.

The third set of priorities given to us in the Lord's Prayer are:

6. Sustain your physical life by working diligently and responsibly.
7. Sustain your spiritual life by pursuing your passions and unifying them with God's will.
8. Forgive others as God forgives you for when your priorities are off-balance.

REFLECT

- Do you feel you have a healthy work-life balance?
- Are you happy with your work?
- Do you worry about financial burdens? If so, what steps are you able to take to become economically stable?
- How often do your responsibilities intrude into your quest for personal fulfillment?
- How do you react when forced to do something you'd rather not do, but know is right?
- Do you have someone in your life who needs your forgiveness? Pray for and forgive that person.

PRAY

Thank you, Jesus, for creating within me a fire to manifest your love through my personal acts of virtue. I know you have given me a mission to complete and the tools necessary to complete it. Teach me how to advance your kingdom as only you know how so that my line in the story of salvation will echo throughout eternity. Amen.

DAY 10

Lead Us Not into Temptation:
You Can't Do This Alone

Lead us not into temptation, but deliver us from evil.

When we first began the Lord's Prayer, I mentioned Thomas Aquinas's quote that when we pray this prayer, "not only do we ask for all that we may rightly desire, but also in the order wherein we ought to desire them." Broken down into its simplest form, the Lord's Prayer places God first, others second, and ourselves third. Once our work for God, our service toward others, and our individual work are complete, there is one final state we are left to experience — that of relaxation.

We all need rest from the thousands of things that call for attention every day. When schedules are overloaded, we tend to do more harm than good. Our outlook on life becomes dark, we become anxious, and we lash out at others due to fatigue and impatience. Without recharging our batteries, we become empty vessels, too weak to carry out our work the way God intended. This makes it impossible to give to others energy, time, and care, because we have neglected to give to ourselves. Even our all-powerful God rested on the seventh day of creation!

That's why it is so important to make sure you rest. If you

are not operating at full capacity, you cannot give to others what they need from you to become happy, holy, and successful. You need downtime to survive. You need to relax to survive.

Here's the thing though: free time is when temptations typically occur. When in a relaxed state and no longer occupied with our work, we are tempted to supplement our souls with an added form of happiness beyond the satisfaction of worship of God, service to others, and individual work. Yes, we are wired to achieve the fulfillment of our souls in God, but we are kind of in a void when we relax. We don't exactly know what to do with ourselves. We drop our guard. As a result, our will is challenged to commit sin as a means to fill this void.

For example, you might be tempted to turn on your laptop and look at porn. That's lust.

You might pull out a pack of cookies and eat the whole thing. That's gluttony.

Perhaps your loved ones invite you out to lunch, but you decide to stay home glued to the television watching game shows as you check social media during commercials. That's sloth.

Now, this isn't to say that all of our motivations for these acts are evil in themselves. Our sexual desire is not bad. On the contrary, the complete giving of one's self to one's spouse within the Sacrament of Matrimony is one of the greatest expressions of love. When sexual desire is deformed into the perversion of porn viewing, though, that's when it becomes lethal to our souls.

The same goes for overeating and watching game shows. Eating, being entertained by a show, or even playing a game are, of course, great ways to nourish the soul. Saint Thomas Aquinas confirms that downtime can be made holy: "Now such like words or deeds wherein nothing further is sought than the soul's delight, are called playful or humorous. Hence it is necessary at times to make use of them, in order to give rest, as it were, to the soul."[11] But eating more than what is needed and

---

[11] Thomas Aquinas, *Summa Theologica*, I-II Q. 168, A. 2.

ignoring loved ones so that you can watch television or play games is dangerous for your health and detrimental to your soul.

Most people defer to screen usage when they are trying to relax. An article from Brookings Institution aptly titled "How Free Time Became Screen Time"[12] illustrates how our natural means of relaxation has been hijacked by technology over the course of the last decade. They highlight a study from the Bureau of Labor Statistics that stated that of all leisure and sports activities undertaken by U.S. citizens ages fifteen and older, screen use averaged a bit more than three hours per day. In contrast, relaxing and thinking averaged just twenty minutes; reading for personal interest twenty minutes; and socializing and communicating with others face to face forty minutes. When you add our screen usage during work and school hours, our minds are fixated on screens almost five times more than they are on the natural world. As a result, we have less time to relax, to ponder, to simply be.

This absence of silence amidst the constant sights and sounds caused by the outside world and our devices has obstructed our ability to delve deeper into God's truths. According to Romano Guardini, author of the book *The Lord*, "The greatest things are accomplished in silence — not in the clamor and display of superficial eventfulness, but in the deep clarity of inner vision; in the almost imperceptible start of decision, in quiet overcoming and hidden sacrifice. Spiritual conception happens when the heart is quickened by love, and the free will stirs to action."[13] It is in the moments of silent contemplation with Our Lord that we come to this spiritual conception which guides us toward the acts that define us as children of God.

Screens act as catalysts toward sin more than virtue. In fact, the majority of the priests and ministers that I interviewed

---

[12] "How Free Time Became Screen Time," Brookings, September 13, 2016, https://www.brookings.edu/blog/social-mobility-memos/2016/09/13/how-free-time-became-screen-time/.
[13] Romano Guardini, *The Lord* (Washington: Regnery Publishing, 1954).

while doing research for this book indicated that the number one obstacle their congregations face when pursuing holiness is the internet.

Young people come to them with problems in their relationships because social media has played such a huge role in their inability to connect with others. Adolescents and adults often are seeking wisdom on how to escape pornography addictions. Men and women of all ages ask for advice on how to properly fast from their devices in order to grow closer to God and their communities.

As technology becomes more advanced, it takes on a greater presence in our lives. As a result, we become more dependent on it, which places us constantly at the threshold of living a more efficient life and a more distracted one.

Before being delivered from evil, we must be cognizant of how the devil tempts us when we turn on these devices. God gives us time to rest and relax so that we can build up our endurance and complete the tasks he gives us in our daily work, our home lives, and our passions. If we are so overworked that we neglect our own health, we deny his life-giving gift of rest; hence, we cannot give what we first do not have. On the other end of the spectrum, we must not take too much from our free time. We must limit the things we do during free time in both quantity and degree, and that includes most especially screen time. We cannot overindulge during this time lest we become the worse for it.

Instead of turning on your device, read a book, sit on the porch and write your thoughts, have dinner with your family, play board games, build a puzzle, or simply praise God for the marvelous life he has given you. Be not led into temptation; be delivered from evil.

Be.

In short, rest responsibly.

Let's Review

The Lord's prayer can be summed up in the following list of priorities:

1. Working for and with God is the first priority.
2. Working in service toward others is second.
3. Working to ensure you thrive on a personal level is third.
4. Once all your work is complete, recreation is your fourth priority.

It is only when your priorities are in this order that you can truly attain your potential for personal excellence. Your phone can both aid in the process and hinder it. It is up to you to decide what activities you choose to partake in concerning your phone. I hope that every time you unlock your screen it is to advance to a higher state of knowledge, wisdom, efficiency, and organization for your life. However, if you are not regulating screen use to achieve these, it is likely that you are becoming less than what you should be.

As you continue on your journey toward detachment from your phone, consider using the Lord's Prayer to counter temptations. Recite it slowly so that you can reflect on the priorities that our life should entail: God, others, work, recreation, and rest.

REFLECT

- Aside from using your phone, what other temptations do you struggle with?
- According to Thomas Aquinas, the Lord's Prayer tells us what we need in the order that we need it. It begins with God and ends with evil. If you were to place your soul on the spectrum that connects the beginning and the end of the prayer, would you consider yourself to be closer to our Father, or evil? Why?

- What things do you do for recreation?
- Do you intentionally get enough rest to refill energy levels and perform to the best of your ability the next day?
- How will you spend your free time today?

PRAY

My Lord, you created a paradise for humanity when you created existence. To this day I experience the joys of this paradise in my times of work, recreation, and rest. May my life be sanctified in both my work and my play so that you may be glorified in all that I do. Amen.

DAY 11

Your True Passion: What Gives You Energy?

God has a plan for your life. He needs you to complete a mission for him. If you complete it, you will be eternally joyful both in this life and the next. This mission may be something ordinary, like pursuing a life dedicated to serving your community, or loving your spouse and children if you are blessed to have them. Or your mission might be something much larger, like creating a worldwide organization that promotes social justice and serving the poor. Either way, God needs you to fulfill your potential of individual excellence by pursuing his mission and completing it to the best of your ability; it is a matter of (supernatural) life or death!

The best part is that when God created you, he placed within you a combination of talents and drive that is unique to your mission. As I mentioned on day 9, this positive desire is called our passion, and when you embrace it fully, you feel a satisfaction that every other aspect of your life simply cannot give you. You might work a day job that pays the bills and provides you with a sense of achievement. Your work makes you feel safe and secure because of the economic stability it provides. When you go home, you are surrounded by a different form of security in your loved ones. With them, you might feel a sense of togetherness and intimacy that all but completes you. To add the icing on the cake, you might even have some free time to dabble in a hobby or two, which keeps you entertained and pleased.

Beyond all of these, however, exists your passion. It beckons to your soul constantly and calls you to become better than you currently are. It satisfies your longings more than your day job, more than your hobbies, and even more than your closest loved ones. It finds its way to rise to the top of your mind and then overtakes your heart because God himself is the primary mover of its existence. He wants you, all of you. He needs you to act on your positive passion because when you do, you'll become more like him. As a result, you'll be perfectly prepared to carry out his mission for your life, a mission that is uniquely tied to your passion.

You might be thinking: "If doing God's will is so important, then why isn't it clear and easy? With God on my side, shouldn't I know what my mission is, and shouldn't I be able to do it with ease? Why do I feel so lost? What actually is my mission? More importantly, what exactly is my passion?"

These are fair questions. In fact, they are the perfect questions to begin your mission! They are the preliminary questions that everyone should ask themselves when they first accept God and begin to follow him faithfully. True Christians have an intense desire to please God, and the first question to ask ourselves after falling in love with him is the same as the rich man who approached Jesus in the Gospel of Luke, "What shall I do to inherit eternal life?" (Lk 18:18).

Jesus' answer tells us what must occur if we desire eternal happiness — follow the commandments, which the man claims to have done since his youth. Jesus then says, "One thing you still lack. Sell all that you have and distribute to the poor, and you will have treasure in heaven; and come, follow me" (v. 22).

The rich man went away sad because he had many possessions. We never find out if he did as Jesus said, we only know that his emotion led him to tears as he walked away from the Truth — that is, Jesus. Did he wake up the next morning ready to sacrifice his treasures? We don't know.

Jesus' plan often differs from our own. This is why we feel so lost. What we want isn't what will make us happy. What God wants for us, however, will. This cognitive dissonance creates within us a confusion that must be overcome. If it's not, we will not fulfill the potential of our personal excellence. On the contrary, we will wade in the waters of mediocrity. We will be lukewarm souls that are neither hot nor cold and, consequently, spat out of the mouth of God for not having pursued his will.

We must, therefore, unite our will with God's if we want to fulfill our missions. Without his help, we will fail; with it, we are guaranteed to succeed. Either way, it's going to take a heck of a lot of effort to accomplish all that he desires us to do.

A good first step toward uniting our will to God's is to eliminate the unnecessary time-wasters in our day, replacing them with contemplation and prayer.

Contemplation refers to the act of thinking deeply about the essence of a particular thing, moment, feeling, or thought. When we contemplate, we delve deep into the foundation of existence in order to comprehend the reason for its being — namely, God. To contemplate, therefore, is to seek what is really true within the thing being observed so as to understand how it fits into the tapestry of creation. In other words, it is to stand side by side with God in order to look upon his creations as the works of art they are while he, the Master Artist, reveals to you in greater detail how he created them to lead all of humanity into endless joy in heaven.

When you are linked to God through consistent and constant contemplative prayer, you will be given the grace of clarity regarding what you are supposed to do with your life. You begin to see your life and the lives of others through God's eyes, and you picture every act as a stone thrown into the pond of this world, creating ripples which travel on into eternity. With this mindset, you are better equipped and divinely fortified to pursue your passion with relentless zeal and fervent gusto.

One of the key benefits of pursuing our passion as provided by God is the added grace of the energy to complete them. In fact, our passions typically give us more energy than they take away. It is not uncommon for runners to wake up early in the morning for training. Many claim that working out at this time of day leads to higher energy levels for the remainder of the day and an increase in self-confidence. On a similar note, many authors stay up into the wee hours of the night scribing their next bestselling novel. Their physical weariness is trumped by their mental focus to the point that they forget about space and time and are so lost in their story that they surround themselves with the settings and the characters of their plots. It is like they have become one with their stories, and they can gain sustenance and livelihood from them.

Regardless of whether you are an early bird or a night owl, your passion is an "energy-giver," something you don't mind sacrificing free time for because the satisfaction you feel leads to higher energy levels. This helps you take on the many "energy-drainers" you experience throughout a regular day.

This energy is paramount to completing your mission. Every person in the history of the world who has fulfilled their potential for personal excellence shares one common trait: when faced with unimaginable obstacles, they were able to maintain the necessary energy levels to rise to the next level of greatness. Michael Jordan suffered by spending countless hours in the gym perfecting his basketball skills. Martin Luther King Jr. suffered mental, emotional, and physical attacks on his family until he paid the ultimate price when he was assassinated. Jesus Christ withstood agony in a garden, scourging at a pillar, carrying of a cross, and crucifixion before emptying his body and soul for the salvation of the world.

How far are you willing to go to pursue your passion? What are you willing to sacrifice?

A good first step is to start small, eliminating unnecessary time wasters and replacing them with the energy-giving act of contemplation and prayer. The simplest method of prayer consists of opening your heart to God and telling him all that is on your mind. Once you've finished, it is even more important to spend time in silence so as to listen to his voice as it manifests itself most often in an inaudible way — usually through a mental connection, a unique thought, a sense of peace, or an experience shortly after your prayer has been made. Everything in life can be a distraction to your mission except prayer. When you are in communication with God, be it in the silence of your heart or through the recitation of prayers, Scripture readings, study, or song, you can only increase in holiness. For a more detailed explanation on how to pray, including instructions on the various types of prayer, visit detachedlife.com.

We know that the rich man had already fulfilled his preliminary mission of following the commandments and living a good life. He was known by Jesus to be a good man, but when one's soul comes face to face with Jesus in faith, being good isn't enough. He wants you to be great, and the requirements to achieve greatness are attaining a zealous prayer life and the ability to succeed in the mission God has given you.

REFLECT

- What activities give you energy?
- What is your passion?
- How much are you willing to sacrifice to pursue your passion in the long run?
- What is keeping you from doing the things you love to do?
- How can you develop a plan to start living the life you've always wanted to live?

PRAY

God, I am in the place that you have brought me to. I know this is not my final destination and that this journey toward you will be filled with peaks and valleys. Be my surety. Make me not arrogant during my times of joy nor distraught during my moments of sorrow. May all of these form me into the perfect being you created me to be. Amen.

DAY 12

The Interior War: Resistance

When one first sows the seed of faith and truly believes in God, that person then seeks understanding, or reasons to believe. The great thing about this is that God himself wants you to understand him too; he wants you to grow closer to him so that the two of you can become one.

Imagine when a young man wants to court a woman. Once the man falls in love with the woman, he will do everything he can to study her and please her. If she likes him back, she will return her love to him in similar gestures. Their relationship becomes a two-way transfer of one giving love to the other, a constant give-and-take with only the other's happiness in mind.

Our relationship with God is similar. We seek reasons for faith in him and thus study his ways intellectually and aim to please him through virtuous actions. God bestows upon us grace, which helps us grow closer to understanding him. The two-way traffic of our faith going toward heaven and his grace coming down to our human existence lifts us up to divine heights and then brings us down to serve others. The Book of Psalms drives this point home: "Mercy and faithfulness will meet; / righteousness and peace will kiss each other. / Faithfulness will spring up from the ground, / and righteousness will look down from heaven" (Ps 85:10–11).

Our persistence in gaining knowledge of God through reason, and our practical application of this knowledge in our lives, create the sides of a ladder on which the rungs of knowledge are added. Step by step, we rise until we've reached the highest point possible of our human existence, which is to see God, who satisfies our every longing. This is why Saint Paul wrote, "For God is at work in you, both to will and to work for his good pleasure" (Phil 2:13).

So, how do we build this ladder? How can we construct it so that it will sustain us and allow for God to shower his grace upon us, especially when we miss a step or want to climb higher than we are capable? The answer is intentional, contemplative prayer. It might sound like a simple thing to do, but in all truth, it isn't.

Regardless of where you are in your faith journey, there are two guaranteed results that will occur when establishing an intentional, contemplative prayer life: you will understand God's mission for your life, and you will be motivated to complete this mission through the use of your talents and passions.

However, there is a challenge when making our climb up the ladder toward true happiness. This challenge comes in the form of resistance, and it causes us to become less than what God has planned for us.

In the book *The War of Art*, dedicated almost entirely to defining, recognizing, and defeating resistance in our artistic lives, author Steven Pressfield defines this awful nuisance: "Resistance cannot be seen, touched, heard, or smelled. But it can be felt. We experience it as an energy field radiating from a work-in-potential. It's a repelling force. It's negative. Its aim is to shove us away, distract us, prevent us from doing our work." His thoughts on the topic also apply to our spiritual lives, perhaps more so than our artistic lives, because when we are no longer attached to the Creator, we are left without the ability to truly create.

Our work, here, is that of our labor for the Kingdom. The devil is constantly distracting us from our mission in many ways because he knows that it will end in our salvation. Resistance, therefore, keeps us from doing our work. It keeps us from doing

God's work and, unfortunately, wears many masks.

The first of these is self-doubt. Resistance steps in when we believe that we are incapable of completing the task God has laid on our hearts. We say to ourselves, "But I can barely write an email that makes sense, how am I going to write a novel?" Or "I can't walk up and down the steps without getting winded, there's no way I could ever run a marathon." When this happens, we typically distract ourselves quickly by seeking comfort in our screen life. We abandon all hope of achieving long-term success because it comes at a cost. We ignore the call to greatness because it will take more time and energy than we are willing to give. Then, we satisfy our short-term urge with a few pixels and a couple of finger strokes across the flat reality of our phones.

When we give in to resistance in this way, we are defeated before we even begin. We nip ourselves in the bud and bear no fruit for God's kingdom because we never gave ourselves a chance to grow in the first place.

The prophet Jeremiah struggled with this form of resistance. He made the excuse that he was only a child and therefore couldn't do what God asked of him. He ignored God's own voice and refused guaranteed long-term success because he was unwilling to put in the time and energy required to achieve personal greatness. Instead, he chose to remain a child, doing the things children do, remaining innocent and afraid of doing what needed to be done.

We are like Jeremiah when we choose technology over our calling. We don't want responsibility. We don't want to sacrifice. We fear failure.

Jeremiah's society burned their own children alive as sacrifice to their false god, Baal. Yet, he was willing to remain in this state of fear rather than do God's will. Our screens trap us in a similar horror. While we do not fear that they will kill us (although we could argue that texting while driving and cyberbullying have led to this extreme), they distract our souls to the point of spiritual death. When we access our screens for distraction, we numb our reason and weaken our intellect. This process is far worse than the threat of physical violence because of the eternal repercussions.

If we are strong in faith and zealous in the practice of it, the physical threats we experience cannot touch our souls or our seeking of eternity. However, if our faith is shaken by constant distraction, and God's call to us to become great is drowned out, then we are in trouble. Jesus told us, "Do not fear those who kill the body but cannot kill the soul; rather fear him who can destroy both soul and body in hell" (Mt 10:28).

Jeremiah needed affirmation, strength, and confidence to overcome this fear, to the point that God told him, "For I know the plans I have for you ... plans for welfare and not for evil, to give you a future and a hope" (Jer 29:11). God tells us the same thing regarding our screens. When we choose the pathway of spiritual distraction, which leads to the death of our souls, God is there to tell us there is "a future and a hope."

There is a common phrase: God doesn't call the equipped, he equips the called. When you are given what the world calls "the kiss of the muse" — or, let's define it as it really is, God's mission for you to complete — you cannot wallow in self-doubt. You must do it. God reminds us that he has conquered this form of resistance, which Saint Paul explained in the Letter to the Philippians: "I can do all things in him who strengthens me" (4:13).

A second form of resistance is having multiple responsibilities. I was listening to a radio program recently on which the host, a psychologist, described how many of his patients complain that they are "too busy" in their daily lives, and that they go crazy attempting to live a life they feel is "unfulfilled" and "hectic." He then spoke about how human beings, especially those in well-developed countries, have more free time now than ever before. In the past, most humans spent the majority of their time from age ten until death working twelve to fourteen hours a day in the fields or doing manual labor in order to survive. Everyone would contribute to this survival and, on the rare occasion that there was free time, the community would hold dances and celebrations as well as religious services, which would typically occur on a Saturday night and Sunday morning so that people could have a brief respite from their work. The average workweek consisted in sixty hours of work for basically anyone who could contribute to household chores, fieldwork, and the like. If you didn't work, you might not survive.

Today, many of us (thankfully) do not need to spend so much time working to ensure our survival. Children have an extended length of time for play, and adults work forty-hour workweeks, more or less. We now have an average of four to five hours per day of free time, far more than our ancestors ever had, and yet we still consider ourselves to be "too busy" to live fulfilled lives. This is resistance telling us that our schedules are too full to complete the missions that God gives to us. We fall into this form of resistance when we fill our free time with multiple, unnecessary responsibilities and, as a result, don't get enough sleep; then we think we need to multitask to survive and lose our zeal for life.

Recognizing the immense freedom we have in our free time is a great first step to conquering this resistance. It puts things in perspective and can lead us to seeking and understanding God's will for us. Leo Tolstoy had ten kids and wrote *War and Peace* (among many other titles). If he can create such beautiful art with such a large family to attend to, then we who have much more free time in our daily lives can surely focus on the things of God in an efficient way if we prioritize our responsibilities correctly.

Take a minute to look back at your monitoring app statistics from the time you began this retreat. Compare your minutes of screen usage from when you first began to now. What "extra" things were you overcommitted to? The latest app? Your Facebook feed? Think about how much your free time used to be eaten up by needless activity, but is now focused on something worthwhile, something divine. If this book has done its job, your current focus should be on the happiness that comes from living life as God desires you to live it and less focused on the distractions that provide you with a false sense of joy.

A third form of resistance is procrastination. If you have already overcome self-doubt, and prioritized your life successfully, procrastination becomes resistance's third line of defense. It tells you that whatever you are inspired to do for God can wait until tomorrow, when it will inevitably not occur at all. In our personal ventures, we tell ourselves, "I will start training for that 5K tomorrow; I've got plenty of time." Or, "I'll write the first chapter in that novel I've been wanting to write in a couple of days; I need to think about it until then and plan it out in my head." Saint Paul would argue that you are wrong, "for you yourselves know well that the day of the Lord will come like a thief in the night" (1 Thes 5:2).

God has placed you in the midst of the fields. His people require your talent. You are a living stone being built into his kingdom, and when you procrastinate, you are like the worker who takes extensive breaks, only to watch those who are getting their hands dirty complete your tasks. If you've ever worked with someone like that, you know that it can be difficult trying to complete your own work because you aren't receiving the help you need. Worse yet, if you've ever been focused on completing a task with someone, but that someone is glued to the phone while you do all of the work, you get twice as upset. God's kingdom is no different, and there is much work to be done, right now — not tomorrow or the next day, but now. He can't have you distracted or putting off his work any longer. He needs you RIGHT NOW.

Resistance wears many masks, and these are just a few of thousands more. The point here is that you recognize that the devil has limitless ways of distracting us from our ultimate goal of knowing, loving, and serving God. Therefore, we must begin work on overcoming resistance on the interior level. If we don't weed it out, it will overcome us, and we will never bear fruit in the way that God has planned. We must tend our spiritual garden before it is too late. Resistance will destroy our souls if we don't do something about it.

The first battle you must wage is that of your unhealthy attachment to your screen.

REFLECT

- What keeps you from realizing your personal excellence?
- What excuses have you made to avoid going all in for God?
- Who are the people who see to it that you are becoming the man or woman that God created you to be?
- What role does your phone play in your relationship with resistance?

PRAY

God, there are obstacles barring me from knowing, loving, and serving you perfectly. Give me the strength and courage to remove them so that I can run quickly to your embrace. May every act of sacrifice be like a battle won in this war that the enemy rages against my soul. May your crushing fist fall upon him and enliven my spirit to fight diligently for the salvation of many. Amen.

DAY 13

Triggers: Recognizing Your Temptations

Last summer I spent months as a stay-at-home dad. I'm a teacher by trade, so those summer moments were ones I cherished with family. However, life became quite busy, as you might imagine. In fact, when I was awake, I was usually a blur of activity, always opting to play with my children, read them books, prepare their meals, and clean up their messes. Since I was writing this book, I would often await my children's bedtime with sleepy anticipation, much like you would await the countdown on New Year's. But when the moment would finally arrive, and all the little ones were far away in dreamland, I collapsed on the couch and reached for my favorite mode of relaxation — my phone.

This wasn't the first time, however, that I had reached for a device during those summer days. While my one- and two-year-olds were taking naps, I was reading breaking news on my tablet. Shortly after they woke up, I was in the playroom watching videos with my four-year-old because she was upset that the two-year-old didn't share his toys. Later, the other children became upset, so they left their toys on the ground and started grabbing for the device. I took out two other tablets and let each of my children navigate a reading app while I began cleaning up the toys. I realized this was a great moment to go to the bathroom, so I left my youngest two glued to their screens and slowly closed the door to the bathroom and took out my phone to check social media. I had already seen the latest posts because, while I was preparing the children's meals throughout the day, I had been checking during the one- to two-minute intervals during which the food was being microwaved. Nothing was new, and as I scrolled down to yesterday's feed, I heard a cry from one of my children. Since I had been done using the bathroom for several minutes, it took me almost no time at all to close my phone, finish up in the bathroom, and attend to the cries of my son. Apparently his tablet had run out of battery, and he was attempting to find the cable from upstairs to recharge it. Unfortunately, he had fallen pretty hard onto the floor after tripping over the cable he was coming down the stairs with. He would be okay, but he needed some daddy hugs ASAP.

Now, as the children were asleep, I was beginning to regain energy as I found myself in the middle of an online game interacting with other users from all around the world. My wife lay beside me watching television. She asked me about my day with the kids, and I looked up every couple of seconds to respond abruptly. Since I wasn't reciprocating any questions, she decided to tell me about her day and how she ran over four miles in preparation for a 10K. While she told me the news with great excitement, I gave her a halfhearted hug and went back to my game.

My wife wanted to share her joy with me, but she saw I was glued to my screen and imagined that I must have had a long day. She decided not to say anything to me about my ignoring her for my device. She too has been guilty of too much scrolling in the evenings after long days, so she thought to herself, "Who am I to tell him to log off and talk with me when I do the same thing?" So she kissed me on my forehead, told me she loved me, then went to wash the dishes, because it was likely they wouldn't get done that night otherwise. She decided to go to bed early so she could be fresh and ready for another run in the morning.

I, on the other hand, stayed up later than I wanted. I didn't fall asleep until I had responded to all of my emails and then did a little online shopping. Two hours had passed in what I thought was only a few minutes. Noting the late time, I rustled into the bed where my wife had already fallen asleep. I lay down with my eyes wide open and my legs restless. I had been exhausted when the children went to bed at 8:00 p.m., but now that it was time for me to sleep, I couldn't. I was tired, but something kept my body alert while I tossed and turned in bed. I remembered then that I had originally planned to spend an hour writing another chapter in the book I started a few months ago.

That's when my six-month-old woke up for his 2:00 a.m. feeding.

I, like most of the world, have a behavioral addiction to my screen. I am frustrated at the end of the day because I don't feel as if I ever get a moment to myself — and I'm right. Every second of my day is accounted for as my attention is given freely to my children, my wife, and the millions of users that dwell behind the screen I view. If there is a brief moment of downtime, it is given to my loved ones or to satisfying my digital fix.

My frustrations are caused by what is known as a trigger. Triggers are situational circumstances where we find ourselves attempting to fulfill a desire for happiness in the face of indifference, sadness, and/or boredom.

As mentioned earlier, humans are hard-wired to experience happiness on the highest scale by doing whatever they feel necessary to establish that happiness. Most equate this with some sort of emotional or sensorial activity such as eating, drinking, making love, etc. When we participate in these activities, we receive a hit of dopamine that causes our brains to surge with elation and satisfies our desire for happiness for a brief period, but when the experience is over, we are left with the same indifference, sadness, and/or boredom that we started with. So we naturally repeat these experiences, usually with higher doses, to maintain our elation and sustain it for longer periods of time. After multiple repetitions, we find ourselves unable to free ourselves from the hooks of our behavior; hence we are addicted to the dopamine hits that they provide us. What seemed like a good idea to cure a short-term issue eventually turns into a long-term addiction.

An often overlooked attribute of triggers is that they coincide within a specific context that, when eliminated, or at least regimented, can disarm the trigger before we even have contact with it. For example, a substance addict can take the first steps toward overcoming his addiction by eliminating the contexts in which he finds himself using drugs. An alcoholic, for example, can avoid the bar, skip the alcoholic beverage section at the store, or even move to another town where he can create new friendships that aren't like his current ones that pressure him to drink on a regular basis.

Internet addicts, however, don't have this ability. We live in a world where we need to be connected if we want to survive. There are very few jobs that exist in which you don't need to provide your email address on your résumé. To top it off, everywhere we go we see people fully engaged in the online activity of the day. The online addict must operate in the context of his or her own addiction all the time. This makes this addiction difficult, almost impossible, to overcome, especially if he or she lacks the willpower to accomplish it. The gaming addict, the binge shopper, the blogger, and the social-media poster are all triggered by the very presence of their devices. When the push notification sounds and the screen lights up, our dopamine levels rise and our curiosity is piqued.

All addictions, then, begin with a trigger that presents itself as the answer to short-term problems. When we experiment with these triggers, we find ourselves walking down a dangerous path toward addiction. The key to overcoming this long and lonely road to destruction is to recognize the triggers before it's too late and remove ourselves from the contexts that bring about our negative behaviors.

So, what's your trigger? I've provided a starter list to help you recognize the spark that leads to your online use.

Triggers Caused by Indifference or Boredom
- When you are waiting for food to cook
- Waiting in lines

- When you're stopped at a red light
- When you do not want to engage with your children
- When you're at a coffee shop or restaurant
- During commercial breaks while watching television
- When you want to know some trivial fact
- When you're a passenger in a car, bus, plane, or boat
- When you have the day off
- When the book you are reading is boring
- When you're going to the bathroom

Triggers Caused by Sadness/Loneliness

- When you're not on speaking terms with loved ones
- After the death of a loved one
- Economic instability
- When you cannot perform at work or in school
- When your children are away from home
- When you need a friend to talk to
- When you've gone through a breakup
- When you doubt your faith
- When you're exhausted
- When you're hungry
- When you have too much going on
- When you're stressed
- When you feel like you should be doing something else with your life
- When your heart says one thing, but your brain says another

Granted there are many more that I haven't listed. Feel free to write those that are unique to you in the margins of this book. In fact, I hope you do because the point of listing these triggers is to call attention to them, to bring them to the surface of your thoughts, so that you can properly defend yourself from them when the time comes. If you defeat these triggers, you will avoid becoming hooked and your addiction will become weaker and weaker. When you finally defeat your addiction, you'll be able to give your complete attention to your loved ones, you'll have that moment for yourself to pursue your passion, and you'll be able to fall asleep comfortably each night. Your life won't be perfect, but it will be meaningful, just as soon as you can disarm your triggers. I will show you how to do that in tomorrow's chapter.

REFLECT

- What is/are your trigger(s) to use your phone?
- Do you find yourself realizing that you have these triggers but ignoring the desire to resist them?
- Have you ever tried to hide your screen use from loved ones by sneaking into the bathroom or another place that blocked their view of you?
- Do you ever feel guilty when using your phone in the presence of others?
- Do you try to "escape" from your life by using your phone to avoid conversations with others, work, and other responsibilities?

PRAY

God, every breath I take, every starlit night, every sunrise, every meal, and every loving embrace comes directly from you. You trigger me at every moment of my existence. When I am tempted to grab my phone during times of boredom or struggle, may I turn to you first and recognize the beauty you have placed not only in the world but in the daily occurrences of my life. Amen.

DAY 14

The Alternative: Replacing Your Tech Time

As I prepared to write this book, I researched several different apps that would monitor my online activity, specifically on my phone. I had heard that using them would give me a better perspective on how often I unlocked my phone, how much time I spent on my screen, and how much time I was using each individual app on a daily basis. I downloaded a few different apps and, while they were installing, I took a guess as to how much time I was dedicating to tech usage. I hypothesized that I was viewing the digital world for about forty-five minutes each day.

I remember the events of that first night with almost perfect clarity. My wife was away from the house at an event for her work, and I was home with our four young children. We were downstairs as I downloaded the apps at around 6:00 p.m. as the children were playing around me. Every few minutes, one or two would try to engage me, but I would say, "Just a minute, hon, daddy has to finish this real quick." It didn't take long before they realized that I would be absent from their play, so they fended for themselves as I delved deeper into my research.

At the end of the night, I managed to detach myself long enough to get the kids ready for bed: I fed them an evening snack, helped them brush their teeth, said evening prayers, and tucked them in. They were sound asleep by 9:00 p.m., and my wife was still at her event, so I sat on the couch and took a look at my results: two hours and thirty-six minutes!

I couldn't believe it. I had just downloaded the monitoring app three hours ago. How was it possible that I was on my screen for two hours and thirty-six minutes? Then the tough questions came: What did I miss out on with my kids? Did I ignore their needs to the point of neglect? What kind of father am I? What example am I giving them? Will they grow up to be addicts like me?

The worst part about it is that even after I realized how much my screen attachment was ruling my life at home and work, I couldn't put it down. For the remainder of the month, the monitoring app indicated I was spending more than three hours per day on the phone. No matter how hard I tried, I simply could not get away. There was always an email to respond to, a post to like, a video to watch, a survey to take, or a text to send. I was hooked.

Earlier in this book, I talked about how the "hooks" that are the gateways to our behavioral addictions with screens are rooted in the seven deadly sins. While I'd love to make a similar comparison and show that each hook has a specific virtue as its counterpart, I simply cannot do it.

Virtues are a "habitual and firm disposition to do the good. It allows the person not only to perform good acts, but to give the best of himself. The virtuous person tends toward the good with all his sensory and spiritual powers; he pursues the good and chooses it in concrete actions." (*Catechism of the Catholic Church*, 1803). In other words, a virtuous life goes beyond our screens. It is a lifestyle that manifests itself in every thought, word, and deed within us. Virtues are not counterparts to anything; they are the foundations of everything that is good, true, and beautiful.

A virtuous life begins with focus. Focus isn't a goal; it is a system, a lifestyle that one adopts if one desires to live freely. When attached to screens, we become a slave to them. The power button and Wi-Fi connection are shackles, and the hook followed is the master. Whatever that hook may be — email, social media, gaming, porn — if it distracts us from higher priorities, it will consume us and make us less than what we are meant to be. It destroys the potential for personal excellence and turns us into a cog in the man-made system of the internet. As Socrates once wrote: "The truly free individual is free only to the extent of his own self-mastery. While those who will not govern themselves are condemned to find masters to govern over them."

You have the power to become the master of your domain. Man's dominion over nature and his own will has been part of our divine makeup since the beginning of time:

> God said: "Let us make man in our image, after our likeness; and let them have dominion over the fish of the sea, and over the birds of the air, and over the cattle, and over all the earth, and over every creeping thing that creeps upon the earth." So God created man in his own image, in the image of God he created him; male and female he created them. And God blessed them, and God said to them, "Be fruitful and multiply, and fill the earth and subdue it; and have dominion over the fish of the sea and over the birds of the air and over every living thing that moves upon the earth." (Gn 1:26–28)

The question then, is, How do I become the master of my own domain? The answer is simple to understand, but difficult to put into practice.

First, you must replace your triggers with a higher priority. More often than not, we are tempted to use our devices when we have another, higher-priority task pending. For example, I should probably be cooking dinner, spending time with my family, finishing up some things for work, and/or doing something that will actually make me feel accomplished. With all of these looming over my head, I can easily escape them with the press of a button. I dive into the digital world and come out at the last minute, if I'm lucky, shortly before my pending responsibilities consume me. Most of the time I'll scratch off one or more of those higher priorities to free up screen time, which ends up in incomplete tasks, stress, personal failure, and/or ordering pizza because I burnt our dinner again.

To avoid the eternal scroll that leads to your demise, you need to nip it in the bud right off the bat. Do this by giving each looming task a value based on the list of priorities from earlier in this book. For example, using my description from above, I would force myself to accomplish those tasks in the following order:

1. Cooking dinner is priority because it corresponds to maintaining the health of my family.
2. Spending time with my family because the needs of my loved ones must come before my own.
3. Finishing up things for work because it maintains the security and sustenance of my household.
4. My passion, although it affects those around me least, because I am driven to complete it through God's inspiration constantly working within me.

If all of these tasks are complete, then and only then, should I feel comfortable using my screen for entertainment, to communicate with friends and family, or simply to cure boredom. If I am checking email or getting the high score in an addictive game before the plates are washed and the kids are put to bed, odds are I won't finish all that I've been given to do.

Another way to alert yourself to screen use is to replace your home screen with an image that will remind you of your priorities. I have my God's Wi-Fi image, with the cross emitting wavy lines to represent the Wi-Fi signal, on all of my devices. This reminds me that when I use them, I must only use them in a way that will help me achieve my full potential.

I can do that only if priorities are in order and if all the tasks I have to complete in those priorities are taken care of. If one act is withheld from the list, I've undermined my own success.

Replace tech time with life. Every time you feel the urge to grab your device, think about your higher priorities and engage yourself first in the tasks that God has set before you. Don't let yourself become distracted by your screen, but rather make yourself aware of just how much your Christian spirit and God-given talents are needed in your home, at work, and in the world. With you, the fruits of your labor can be so much more. Without your complete attention to the life you were meant to live, the world becomes so much less.

REFLECT

- What does your mind focus on at any given moment during the day?
- How can you become master of your domain when it comes to screen use?
- At what point does your phone use cease to be leisure time and become addictive behavior?
- With what activities will you replace your tech time from here on out?

PRAY

Heavenly Father, you have given me so many opportunities to better myself and those around me. Time and again I fail to take advantage of these opportunities, and yet you forgive me for my weakness and encourage me to rise again, stronger in my hope to please you. Grant me the desire to pursue you with the ardent zeal of the saints, so that I may one day celebrate with them in your celestial court. Amen.

DAY 15
Contemplation: The Life Force of the Soul

When I was a kid I had a pair of Superman pajamas with a Velcro cape that attached to my shoulders. At five years old I truly believed I had superpowers as long as I had it on. I'd use my super strength to lift boxes of Styrofoam that were three times my size; I'd use my super speed to cover the terrain of my backyard and guard the house from approaching butterflies. My most daring feat was to jump from the top of the couch and fly through the air before falling gently onto the beanbag chair below. I was convinced that I was a superhero, and I acted accordingly.

My brothers, on the other hand, were archenemies. While I was busy defending our household from bugs entering our fortress of solitude, they would sneak up behind me with the stealth of a mite and rip my cape off. Then they would put it back on my shoulders backward so that the Superman "S" would be hidden from view. They claimed that this would "reverse my powers" and destroy my abilities.

I was distraught. Naturally I went to mom and dad and cried my eyes out. I'd be comforted by their love and regain my powers as the cape was placed correctly on my shoulders. My brothers, on the other hand, would receive some sort of punishment, none more severe than the laser beams I'd shoot from my wide open and teary eyes when we crossed paths for the rest of the day.

At five years old I knew that there was an ideal that men strived for in Superman. In every man and woman there exists a natural desire to discover perfection in truth. In my case, I sought the perfect physical being that superpowers could provide. My imagination carried me toward a fictional character whose capabilities were greater than mine, and I began to imitate his powers as if they were my own. Superman was a precursor, a type of perfection that I would one day understand to be God.

Our minds extend themselves beyond our own ideals in an attempt to fathom God's reasoning. The problem is, we never arrive at the state of perfection we desire. In much the same way that I attempted to live as if I had superpowers, men and women throughout space and time have longed to be like God by pondering his existence, recognizing his power, imitating his virtue, and living out his divine commands. This method of thinking "like" God is what is known as contemplation, and it is through this intentional act that the real superpower of the human soul — the intellect — is revealed.

As mentioned earlier, the intellect is a power of the soul in which our human ability to reason is stored. Through our reason, we can ponder the greatness of God in our thoughts and see the world through his divine light of truth. C. S. Lewis once wrote, "I believe in Christianity as I believe that the sun has risen: not only because I see it, but because by it I see everything else." Contemplation, then, is the means through which we "see everything else," a manner of thinking that requires our souls to detach from the worldly lures that keep us thinking as men do, not as God does.

While on this earth, we are charged with the mission to pursue God with all of our heart (see Col 3:23). We will never fully understand his ways, for if we could, we ourselves would be God. Rather, as Saint Paul states: "For now we see in a mirror dimly, but then face to face. Now I know in part; then I shall understand fully, even as I have been fully understood" (1 Cor 13:12).

In other words, the work we put in to achieve the fullness of our potential for personal excellence by discovering the ways of God will be thoroughly rewarded when we enter into the fullness of truth at the moment of our death. Our transition from this life into the next will seem like nothing, for we will have been fully integrated into God's love by becoming his most humble of servants during our earthly lives. Again from Saint Paul: "For I am sure that neither death, nor life, nor angels, nor principalities, nor things present, nor things to come, nor powers, nor height, nor depth, nor any other creature, will be able to separate us from the love of God in Christ Jesus our Lord" (Rom 8:38–39). When we arrive in heaven, we shall see God as he is, and our earthly desire to know, love, and serve him will be quenched beyond all human understanding by his divine presence.

Saint Augustine reiterates this truth, "the contemplation of God is promised us as being the goal of all our actions and the everlasting perfection of our joys."[14] Saint Thomas Aquinas refers to this in his *Summa* and explains further by stating, "This contemplation will be perfect in the life to come, when we shall see God face to face, wherefore it will make us perfectly happy: whereas now the contemplation of the divine truth is competent to us imperfectly, namely 'through a glass' and 'in a dark manner' (1 Cor 13:1–2)."[15]

Jesus tells us to "be perfect, as your heavenly Father is perfect" (Mt 5:48). If our superpower is our ability to become perfect, to think as God does through contemplation, then our weakness is anything that distracts us from the act of contemplation.

For most of us, our phones are our kryptonite. They create within us what us known as a "monkey mind," a Buddhist term meaning our thoughts are "unsettled; restless; capricious; whimsical; fanciful; inconstant; confused; indecisive; uncontrollable."[16] Monkey mind spins our intellect into a whirling turbulence that devastates our will and leaves us with an inability to contemplate

---

[14] Augustine of Hippo, *De Trinitate*, I, 8.
[15] *Summa Theologica*, I-II, Q. 180, A. 4.
[16] https://en.wikipedia.org/wiki/Mind_monkey.

God's truths in our lives. We get so caught up in our digital lives that we can't recognize the things that make life worth living.

Saint Thomas tells us, "For the act of contemplation, wherein the contemplative life essentially consists, is hindered both by the impetuosity of the passions which withdraw the soul's intention from intelligible to sensible things, and by outward disturbances."[17] In other words, our desire to see God, to become perfect like him, is squelched by our personal temptations toward lesser things. Be it entertainment, prowess, pride, or lust, our screens cause us to want God less and want our emotions and personal satisfaction more. In short, our phones destroy our ability to reason, which demotes us to the same plane of existence as animals that can only act upon passions for survival and pleasure and have no concept of virtue and truth. We thus attain, quite literally, a monkey's mind.

But there's a way to defeat it. St. James teaches us how to overcome our monkey-mindedness:

> And let steadfastness have its full effect, that you may be perfect and complete, lacking in nothing. If any of you lacks wisdom, let him ask God, who gives to all men generously and without reproaching, and it will be given him. But let him ask in faith, with no doubting, for he who doubts is like a wave of the sea that is driven and tossed by the wind. For that person must not suppose that a double-minded man, unstable in all his ways, will receive anything from the Lord. (James 1:4–7)

To own a cellphone is to be constantly tempted to be "double-minded." Every push notification, every status update, every text message sent and received is a means through which your intellect can be distracted from contemplating perfection. It is only through contemplation that we can truly appreciate the gift that technology can be as opposed to the threat to our souls that it currently is.

---

[17] *Summa*, IHI, Q. 180, A. 2.

God is the creator of all things, and through him all existence is held together (see Col 1:17). Since God is good, created all things, and sustains them in existence, we can logically deduce that all things in existence currently are because God willed them. We can also deduce that every created thing in this world (and the next) has a certain degree of good in it, because if it didn't, God would not will it to exist. Take, for example, the devil himself, the most evil thing in existence. It must drive him absolutely nuts that even he remains in existence through God, his sworn enemy.

Your phone isn't the devil. On the contrary, your phone has an immense potential for good, just as it has an equally immense potential for bad. Everything hinges on your ability to contemplate the good that can be produced through the use of your phone. The thing itself isn't the issue. It is how you choose to use it that makes screen time either a holy encounter or a self-destructive behavior. Aquinas states: "To wisdom belongs first of all contemplation which is the vision of the Beginning, and afterwards the direction of human acts according to the Divine rules. Nor from the direction of wisdom does there result any bitterness or toil in human acts; on the contrary the result of wisdom is to make the bitter sweet, and labor a rest."[18]

So what do you want your phone to be for you? A weapon that unlocks the secrets of divine wisdom, or the kryptonite that weakens your soul and renders you powerless to sinful temptations? You get to choose through the intentional, willing act of contemplation.

REFLECT

- Does your phone bring you closer to God or lead you further away from him?
- How often do you practice contemplation in your daily life?

---

[18] *Summa*, I-II, Q. 45, A. 3.

- What steps can you take to create more time for contemplation every day?
- What benefits do you hope to achieve from instituting a more contemplative lifestyle?

PRAY

Dear Lord, help me understand how wonderful your power is through the secrets you reveal to me in meditation, contemplation, and acts of virtue. May they be the foundation for a life well lived so that my own joy can be my legacy for others to imitate. Amen.

DAY 16

Boredom: Embrace the Act of Being

Maria Montessori, famed educator and expert in child brain development, once said that "play is the work of children." In 2016 the U.S. Department of Health and Human Services estimated that American children spend an average of seven hours a day in front of electronic media, thus replacing a large chunk of their "play" time with consumption of digital media. When multiplied across the entire week, that adds up to forty-nine hours, which is more than an average workweek for an American adult. In essence, then, children are spending more time on their screens than most adults spend on their careers, and the effects on brain development are staggering.

When it comes to recognizing substance addiction in drug and alcohol addicts, scientists have used brain scans and blood samples to determine why users of these dangerous substances constantly return to their use. Substance addicts crave the chemical effects of using, not the substance itself. Every time they consume the dangerous substance, they receive a shot of dopamine that stimulates their cells and gives them a sense of elation and adrenaline. This sense is short-lived, and as it begins to dwindle the user re-ups their dose little by little until their bodies become dependent on the substance for physical and psychological survival. Breaking free from this vicious circle is nearly impossible unless the addiction is caught in its early stages.

These same addictive behaviors are found in children who use screens at an early age. Scientists have discovered that most children exposed to screens at three years old show signs of addiction that are similar to adult substance addicts. Each time they power on a device, they receive that same shot of dopamine which rewards their brains with a short-lived feeling of euphoria. As they scroll, press buttons, and respond to audiovisual stimuli that illuminate the device, the ante is upped and the addictive pattern of dopamine hits builds. When the device loses power or screen time is over, they hit the wall and rebel against the authority that keeps them from their addiction. It can take weeks, even months for their brains to detox from these effects and, even if they do succeed, all other play experiences pale in comparison to screen time.

The addiction doesn't end there. Most teens and adults also hail screens as the be-all and end-all of their entertainment and, as such, find it difficult to enjoy much else. We know that devices can create an objective, tangible form of entertainment with a mere touch of a button and no mental or physical exertion required. So why would we take the extra step of using our minds and bodies to create entertainment for ourselves? That takes time and energy, and, for most people, the process of creating entertainment or consuming stimuli from the natural world — that is, reading books, inventing games, spending time with others, observing nature — has been looked on as remarkably boring. In essence, when given the option of creating our own fun or having devices cure a state of boredom, we are more likely to choose the latter. Thus screens have interrupted our ability to embrace boredom.

Being bored is a natural state of life, one experienced often at every age. As children, we are bored when our brothers and sisters are sick and we have no one to play with. As teens we are bored when we have to go shopping with our mom or when we have to wait for dinner to be prepared. As adults we are bored when there is a lull of activity during work or when we have to stand in line at the bank. Every day boredom comes to greet us with its lethargic apathy, and today we typically respond to boredom by reaching for our phones. The results are harmful to our psyche. As it turns out, we need boredom to survive.

Our brain is always working. During waking hours we are constantly engaged in thought that spans from conscious and intentional activity, such as when you are adding and subtracting numbers to manage your personal budget, to relaxed and free thought, such as walking on the shore of a beach and marveling at a sunset. At any given time during the day your brain may work on the conscious level while focusing intently on the here and now, or it may drift into the subconscious level as you daydream.

Regardless of how much you work your brain, it always continues to work for you. Researchers have discovered that while in a subconscious state of thought — for example, daydreaming — your brain is still working at 95 percent of the same effort it would take if you were attempting to solve a difficult math problem. That means your brain is remarkably productive, even when at rest!

This brainpower is the central nervous system of the spiritual life. According to researcher Jonathan Smallwood, "Daydreaming is an interesting phenomenon because it speaks to the capacity that people have to create thought in a pure way rather than thought happening when it's a response to events in the outside world."[19] These pure thoughts, then, are what creates the foundation for our relationship with God. Freedom of thought builds our capacity to reason. As a result, we are more likely to reason our way into the logical existence of God and thus allow the Holy Spirit to propel our souls into discipleship. When we are lost in thought, we make spiritual connections that are simply impossible when constantly reacting to the stimuli around us.

The philosopher Joseph Rassam wrote that "silence is within us the wordless language of the finite being that, by its own weight, seeks and carries our movement toward the infinite Being."[20] It's in the moments of undistracted silence that we ponder our deepest

---

[19] Quote can be found at https://web.archive.org/web/20180410055526/http://dujs.dartmouth.edu/2011/02/science-of-daydreaming/.
[20] Referenced in *The Power of Silence: Against the Dictatorship of Noise*. Cardinal Robert Sarah, San Francisco: Ignatius Press, 16–17.

thoughts and thus become more closely united to God.

You were meant to be a saint, and to do that you must surrender your thoughts to God, constantly willing to grasp perfection in every act, every thought, and every intention you pursue.

This all starts with how we treat boredom.

Today's culture tells us that Church, and everything related to God — philosophy, theology, catechism class, even serving the poor! — is boring. Whenever someone complains that praying or attending Mass is "boring," I get excited, because boredom is the first step toward entering into the subconscious level of thought that has the potential to connect us with the Creator. With just a glimpse at the stained-glass window, a whiff of burning incense, the tone of the Gospel being read, and the sense of togetherness with the ones you love, the Holy Spirit can work his power and offer so much more than the lures the world can offer — if we can keep our hands away from our phones.

When we reach for our phones during times of boredom, we break the subconscious daydreaming that can lead us toward God, and we substitute it for the conscious reaction to stimuli that the digital world constantly provides. Instead of looking upon our children with pride and wonder as they play on the playground, we like a meaningless image of a kitten. Instead of sitting down for a hot meal with someone we love, we take pictures of our food and eat alone. Instead of awakening our minds to the endless possibilities our lives offer us by philosophizing while we do our business in the bathroom, we scroll endlessly until our legs and souls fall asleep. Instead of calming our minds and entering into the joys of daydreams and supernatural epiphanies, we buy things online that we don't need.

Steve Jobs, the cofounder of Apple and innovator of personal smart devices that now inundate our lives, once said: "I'm a big believer in boredom. … All the [technology] stuff is wonderful, but having nothing to do can be wonderful, too."[21] In fact, Jobs himself refused to let his own children use the devices he had created,

---

[21] "What Boredom Does to You," Nautilus, October 26, 2017, http://nautil.us/issue/53/monsters/what-boredom-does-to-you.

opting instead for them to read books, play games, and, ultimately, to be bored. He boldly chose to raise his children free of iPads, iPhones, and the like because he knew their natural creativity was not something to be squandered. Rather, through benevolent neglect, they could develop skills to entertain themselves, develop empathy toward those around them, and shape their curiosity.

Jobs went on to say that "out of curiosity comes everything." If we truly desire to maximize our potential for personal excellence, we should take a page out of his book and appreciate technology for what it can offer us, but also take bold action in limiting the distractions that cause us to be less than we were destined to be.

When we decrease screen time we will, inevitably, become "bored." How you react to that boredom will define you. With proper discernment of your talents and ample contemplation of the world around you, you will do something truly remarkable with your life; something that will ultimately fulfill God's call to know, love, and serve him in the way you are uniquely created to do.

REFLECT

- Have you ever considered something to be boring that you once thought was actually quite amazing?
- Do you often feel that many aspects of your Christian life are boring?
- Do you think you could be content living your life without the benefits of technology? Would that be prudent given your current state?
- What else makes you bored?

PRAY

God, as Saint Augustine once said, "My heart is restless until it rests in you." This short time of our earthly existence is filled with waiting. We wait in constant anticipation that our desire to know you will be fulfilled on that day of the Beatific Vision. Guide us toward the light of your truth so that we can experience the joy of your living Word on this side of life and the other side of death. Amen.

DAY 17

Dedication: Making Time for Mastery

It has been said that in order to become an expert at any particular skill one has to dedicate a minimum of 10,000 hours to practice. In other words, it takes 1,250 eight-hour days to master a skill. That is the equivalent of 250 work weeks (with no vacation time), nearly five years, of perfecting your abilities.

It has also been said that since technology is increasing at such an exponential rate, many of the skills we will need to "perfect" in order to complete our work and hobbies have not been conceptualized yet. In essence, we are on a constant learning curve where only the pliable, tech-savvy mind can survive. In a world where the only constant is rapid change, the 10,000-hour rule seems a bit outlandish.

So where do we find peace of mind? How can one develop skills that don't exist yet for survival at work, to pursue our passions in an environment that is becoming more digital by the second, and to remain focused on the ultimate mission of fulfilling our desire to know God?

The answer is found in how we manage time.

To do that we have to desire mastery. Without motivation we are destined to become an amateur, mediocre in abilities and unable to fulfill the potential of our personal excellence. When Thomas Aquinas was asked by one of his brothers, "What must

I do to become a saint?" he answered, "Will it." Without the will to detach from everything this world offers us, we cannot attain the spiritual perfection that God requests. We must take up the cross and follow him.

Now, following a spiritual journey does not discount current realities of our present state. Aquinas would argue that it is through the senses that we can come to know, love, and serve God. God created us with both body and soul, which means both faith and reason are meant to guide us, like two wings in a perfectly balanced flight toward divine heights. When scientists and logicians believe that it takes 10,000 hours to perfect a skill, they might actually be telling us something about our souls.

What drives you? What is the passion that God placed within you to complete the mission he has set before you? On day 11 we discussed how important this passion is to your salvation as well as for the souls of those around you. Beyond work, beyond your personal responsibilities, can you safely say that you have dedicated 10,000 hours to mastering your passion?

Anders Ericsson, a Florida State University psychologist whose research on expertise spawned the 10,000-hour rule, once said, "You don't get benefits from mechanical repetition, but by adjusting your execution over and over to get closer to your goal."[22]

"You have to tweak the system by pushing," he adds, "allowing for more errors at first as you increase your limits."[23] In other words, 10,000 hours of merely showing up and "going through the motions" of repeating the same task at the same level of ease doesn't lead to excellence. Development comes from a constant challenge, one that needs to increase in difficulty as the learner grows in aptitude, to complete more complex variations of the skill over the course of time.

For most people this development never occurs because

---

[22] "Dubunking the Myth of the 10,000-Hours Rule: What It Actually Takes to Reach Genius-Level Excellence," brainpickings, https://www.brainpickings.org/2014/01/22/daniel-goleman-focus-10000-hours-myth/
[23] Ibid.

they lack the motivation to pursue it beyond its current worth. They remain amateurs in a skill because it fulfills the needs of survival. Daniel Goleman, in his book *Focus: The Hidden Driver of Excellence*, tells us: "Amateurs are content at some point to let their efforts become bottom-up operations. After about 50 hours of training — whether in skiing or driving — people get to that 'good-enough' performance level, where they can go through the motions more or less effortlessly. They no longer feel the need for concentrated practice, but are content to coast on what they've learned. No matter how much more they practice in this bottom-up mode, their improvement will be negligible."[24] In other words, they coast through life never attempting to go deeper into the perfection of their skill. They are content with mediocrity and the comforts it provides for their lives.

Masters, on the other hand, pursue the struggle. Goleman continues, "The experts, in contrast, keep paying attention top-down, intentionally counteracting the brain's urge to automatize routines. They concentrate actively on those moves they have yet to perfect, on correcting what's not working in their game, and on refining their mental models of how to play the game."[25] It is in the struggle that true masters surge ahead. Christ willingly accepted the constant barrage of hatred from men to the point that he suffered death on a cross, so too must a master work tirelessly against a world which seeks at every opportunity to bring him or her down to its level: mediocrity.

I would argue that there are more people working toward mastery in online gaming, social-media-status updates, and the viewing of pornography than there are people who are pursuing their God-given passion and zeal for souls. The world attempts to immobilize us, to keep us on the ground and force us to "lead a life of quiet desperation" as Henry David Thoreau put it in his timeless classic, *Walden*. God, on the other hand, moves within us freely, draws our souls toward heaven, and calls us to serve

---

[24] "Why the 10,000 Hour Rule Is a Myth," Huffington Post, October 8, 2013, https://www.huffingtonpost.com/2013/10/08/success-book_n_4059506.html.
[25] Ibid.

others so that we can achieve eternal life. This is far greater than a life of quiet desperation. On the contrary, this would be a life of peaceful emancipation.

We are only alive for seventy to ninety years (if we're lucky) and the brunt of those years are taken up by work and life responsibilities. How lucky are we to be the bearers of the Good News using the rest of our free time to develop talents that Jesus himself said could be greater than his own great works (see Jn 14:12–14)? What miracles await the works of our hands? What crosses must we bear in the process?

While it may take 10,000 hours to master a particular skill, it takes an entire lifetime to master the spiritual life. The psalmist tells us that our lives are merely puffs of air, or mere breaths (see Ps 39:5), and Saint James reiterates that we are "a mist that appears for a little time and then vanishes" (Jas 4:14). In other words, if we want to make our lives honorable to Our Lord, we do not have any time to waste.

The shortness of our life demands we unite all our time to mastering our relationship with God and others. That means we must witness to him in our work and through our life responsibilities, in our focus and daydreams, alone and with the ones we serve in love, on our phones and without them. Through him we achieve the fullest potential of our personal excellence. Therefore, we must intentionally dedicate time to spiritual mastery and attain the skills necessary to complete our divine mission — and we must do it before it is too late.

REFLECT

- Do you make time on a consistent basis to further your spiritual life? In what ways?
- Do you intentionally set goals and tangible ways to prove that you are growing in your spiritual life?
- Do you have a spiritual director who can act as your coach and help you reach new spiritual heights?

- Do you feel adequately trained to provide spiritual assistance to others if they were to ask for it?

PRAY

Holy Lord, Saint Paul said you are the Father of compassion and the God of all comfort, who comforts us in all our troubles, so that we can comfort those in any trouble with the comfort we ourselves receive from God (see 2 Cor 1:3–5). Provide me with a clear pathway toward holiness so that I can bring as many people along with me, as we journey together toward you. Amen.

DAY 18

Full Focus: Urgency versus Importance

I consider myself a busy, yet very giving man. I'm always willing to help my family, the members of my community, and especially my church. I'm the guy that everyone calls when they need help, whether to substitute as a lector at Mass, or for the catechism teacher who just went on maternity leave for the rest of the year. If you are in a bind, I'm the guy you can count on to get you out of it.

However, I am married and have four children who are active in sports and school activities. I try to balance spending time with my wife and children, working at my nine-to-five, and serving my parish whenever called to do so. I often have to sacrifice my hobbies like exercising, writing, and watching basketball on television. On top of missing out on some personal-interest activities, I often sacrifice time with my wife and children.

One winter evening, while my family and I were on the way to drop my daughter off at swimming lessons, I received a text message and opened it. After reading it, I reluctantly told my wife, as I viewed my cellphone screen: "I need to go. They need me again. I'm sorry."

This was me before I realized how to prioritize my life. I was happy doing what I believed to be "the things of the Lord."

The problem was that my mind was always geared toward completing other people's tasks. I placed no boundaries between myself, my vocation, and my ministries, to the point that everything blended together in a chaotic misappropriation of time and energy. As a result, I consistently felt overworked, overburdened, stressed, and worried. Worst of all, I felt as if I wasn't doing enough, despite the array of activities I was part of. I couldn't give my entire attention, full energy, or constant focus to just one of the aspects of my life at any given time — I was spread too thin.

I'm sure you've been in the same situation. With hearts bigger than our minds, we take on added responsibilities in much the same way that an eight-year-old consumes Halloween candy — no filter, no self-control, acting on impulse. In situations like this, we often consider it a "holy" impulse, a push of the Holy Spirit to "do God's will." The problem is, it is really our own will and sense of fear of letting anyone down that drives us. Ultimately we have a problem with telling the difference between what is urgent and what is important.

Urgency

When we look at the list of priorities established in earlier chapters, we must understand that the tides of life will not always rise and fall at our bidding. Emergencies will arise, our plans for that particular day will need to be sacrificed, and our minds must shift to concentrate on the immediate need. However, we first need to contemplate whether or not the things we consider urgent are truly emergencies.

Yes, our phones help us feel safe, secure, orderly, and connected with others. Unfortunately, they also have a tendency to endanger our minds, leaving our personal lives insecure, thus disconnecting ourselves from others. Phones create interruptions and unnecessary urgency throughout our day.

Take me, for example. I was planning on dropping my daughter off at swimming lessons, but due to the immediate need of my parish a sense of holy duty overshadowed my responsibilities as husband and father. In a split-second decision, I chose what I thought would be most pleasing to the Lord. I was pressured by urgency, and I chose wrongly.

Importance

Right judgment in discovering the will of God in our lives isn't always as easy as we would like it to be. The various aspects of our lives constantly blend, vying for attention and competing for our energy. It isn't always easy to determine what is important.

That's why it is paramount to establish boundaries in life. Boundaries are what keep each aspect of our lives in order. Think about it like a highway. Multiple lanes divided by lines keep us at a safe distance from other cars, while allowing us to observe them and react to ensure everyone's safety. These other cars represent the people in our lives, the lanes represent the work we do to help them and ourselves, and the speed we go represents the time and energy we can dedicate to this work. We change lanes often, passing by colleagues, family members, and loved ones who are also on this road of life. We know that staying in our lanes and going the speed limit, we will arrive at the final destination of heaven together, and live with God for eternity. The only rules are the rules of the road, which here represent the divine law, asking that we stay within our lanes and not veer onto tempting exits.

All goes well along this highway to heaven until a push notification is received saying, "there's a better way if you take exit 666 to S. Lucifer Drive." Taking our eyes off the road for one second to view that message and the car begins to swerve into the other lanes without us noticing. Within seconds people in other lanes are cut off, and in a last ditch effort to grab the wheel and align our priorities again, we veer completely off the road and crash.

We can't drive in every lane at all times. We can't get distracted. In other words, we can't do everything, no matter how tempting the "urgent" thing in life may be. We must always discern the difference between what is important and what is urgent.

The Cellphone Lane

In order to achieve proper discernment over what is urgent and what is important, we must give our cellphones their own lane. So instead of allowing this device to pull your mind into several different lanes throughout the course of the day, bouncing from work to school to entertainment, etc., why not give a certain amount of time to your phone on a daily basis?

Regulate it. Give it the proper amount of time it deserves. Don't let it be the thing that interrupts your plans by creating sudden urgency with every notification. Don't become a victim to the world's plea to respond instantly to all digital communication. Our lives are already busy and confusing; we don't need another thing to dictate priorities to us.

We need to be the ones that dictate our priorities. We need to be the ones that stay in our own lanes for the proper amount of time, so that we can successfully complete the journey toward salvation. If your phone isn't helping you complete that task, then it is likely you are not giving it its own lane.

Let's unpack that for a minute. What does it mean to give your phone its own lane? How can it be separated from home, work, and entertainment lanes when it is so ingrained in each of those aspects of your life?

The answer is to regulate your time and activity based on priorities. As we discussed earlier, you need to choose the higher priority when making decisions based on what is urgent and what is important.

Think about it like a GPS-mapping app. You plug in a destination so that the GPS will allow you to find the best route possible. The more advanced the app, the more efficient the journey will be — you'll know where accidents have occurred, where the heavy traffic is, and what quicker routes are available according to real-time data. Using your phone in this way speeds up your arrival. It's a perfect way to keep your phone in its own lane, the lane of productivity and efficiency.

There are several other examples to keep your phone in its own lane. Using a banking app can make your banking life easier. You might become better organized by using a planner app or a calendar app. If your phone is used properly, it can make communication with your colleagues, family members, etc., more fluid. Using your cellphone in these productive ways is how you keep it in its correct lane.

God has given us the ability to manage our responsibilities and curb what distracts us from achieving his mission for us in life. Our phones tend to pull our focus away from those goals. As you take the final steps toward completing this retreat, continue to remain focused on the final prize: true detachment from your device. If you have made it this far, it's likely that you have already had a small taste of the effects of detachment. I'm betting you're going to want seconds.

REFLECT

- What do you consider to be on the "urgent" list of your life right now?
- What would you put on the "important" list of your life right now?
- How often does your phone fall into the "urgent" list of your life?

PRAY

God, the only thing that matters in this life is you. You are what I ask for, and the fact that I know you to the point that I am able is a privilege. It is in you that I live in a joy and a happiness that most people will never know or experience outside of the Christian faith. May I be a beacon of light for all so that their salvation and my own might be the most urgent things in my life both now and always. Amen.

DAY 19

Connected: Global Connectivity
versus Retreat to Self

While my children were at an event with my wife recently, I had a few errands to run, so I hopped into the van to begin my journey to the grocery store. When I got there, I found a sea of folks waiting in line to pay for their goods. I took my spot next to a high school boy who had his earbuds in. He was laughing and chuckling and flicked his fingers across his screen, texting multiple times a minute.

I had forgotten my phone at home, so I casually glanced around and saw that I was the only person in the store without my phone. Businessmen stood in their suits, checking their email. A group of girls sat together conversing halfheartedly, leaning over one another to show their screens. A young mother scrolled through her phone while her three-year-old son manically slid his fingertips from side to side while playing a video game on a tablet.

For a moment I was pleasantly delighted to be the only one without a device. I felt unique and free to enjoy the ride. I looked out the store window into the clear morning sky and thought, "What a beautiful day."

Then. I suddenly felt alone. I felt like I was missing out; I wanted to be in on the high-schooler's joke, the girls' screen-sharing spree, the businessman's important emails, and the mother's scrolling. Heck, I wouldn't even have minded playing a video game if the opportunity had presented itself. I wanted to be on my phone looking for personalized entertainment. The high school boy had his music and text-message buddies, but all I had was a destination to arrive at and some groceries to buy. "Boring trip," I thought as I lowered my head, hoping that my phone would magically appear to cure my boredom.

That boredom turned to panic as I realized that, without my phone, I had no way of connecting with my wife and children. What if my wife sent me a message saying we needed something from the store? What if something happens to my children? What if there's an emergency and I need to get hold of them?

When you are addicted, however slightly, the thoughts and feelings associated with not having your cellphone are known as nomophobia. It's a condition that stems from not being able to function without a mobile device. One study from the United Kingdom in 2012, only a few years after smartphones appeared on the scene, found that 66 percent of adults struggle with nomophobia. That number increases the younger you are; for those polled ages twenty-five to thirty-four, 68 percent responded that they were nomophobic. At ages eighteen to twenty-four, those with nomophobia surged to 77 percent.

Technology has become so ingrained in our lives that we live in fear of losing it. This is a telltale sign of behavioral addiction. We validate that addiction because of its normalization throughout society. Everywhere we go, people are glued to screens because, What if there's an emergency? What if we get lost and need GPS? What if we get bored? We loathe the thought of living without the sense of personal security and entertainment phones provide us.

But that's all it is — a sense. It's not a reality.

The reality is that nomophobia leads to other negative effects, none more dangerous than the destruction of human-to-human interaction.

Researchers from the University of Essex found that people

who discussed personally meaningful topics when a cellphone was nearby reported lower relationship quality and less trust in their partner. That same study showed that their partner was also less empathetic to their concerns.[26]

Another study from the University of Maryland found that smartphone use is likely to make us more selfish and more introverted due to a lack of human contact. That same study found that smartphone users were less likely to act intentionally in a way that would benefit another person or society as a whole. As a result, they are less inclined to participate in volunteer activities or to simply help someone in need.[27]

The world is slowly beginning to recognize the downside to technology overuse. A Catholic priest whom I interviewed told me that it is the number one thing he hears in the confessional for both the young people he works with as a college chaplain and the adults he has regular communication with. He said: "They notice that it is affecting their souls. They confess to viewing pornography and spending too much time on social media to the point that they go on these fasts from their phones. They do it because they know there's something dark about it."

There is something dark about it — technology is systematically changing how we interact with one another by claiming to connect us more closely. Unfortunately the opposite effect is occurring — technology has caused us to become more isolated, less empathetic, and less connected with our communities than ever before.

This has caused some serious conversations to arise on the topic of friendships. As we move toward more digital interactions, our interpersonal relationship conversations — meaning those close-knit dialogues we would save for our friends — have started to fall by the wayside. A dangerous side effect is that

---

[26] "Can you connect with me now? How the presence of mobile communication technology influences face-to-face conversation quality," *Journal of Social and Personal Relationships*, July 19, 2012, http://journals.sagepub.com/doi/abs/10.1177/0265407512453827.
[27] "UMD Researchers Find Cell Phone Use Linked to Selfish Behavior," University of Maryland Division of Research, February 16, 2012, https://research.umd.edu/news/news_story.php?id=7145.

many people are choosing to text their friends instead of spending moments together, thereby missing interacting with one another on a vast array of topics such as work, hobbies, love, and God.

In an article from *Relevant Magazine,* writer Lindsay Williams illustrates this point:

> Lasting friendships are built on far more than a Facebook history. They're forged in the fire of life's peaks and valleys. They're held together by more undocumented memories than documented ones.
>
> While social media may help us keep up with friends — especially those who live far away — it can't replace personal communication and shared experience. You can only intimately get to know someone through spending time with them in person, not solely online.[28]

God has placed within us a desire to know, love, and serve him, but he has also ingrained within us an intense need for a community of friends. As G. K. Chesterton wrote, "Because our expression is imperfect we need friendship to fill up the imperfections."[29] The connectivity we feel, then, within our intimate friendship circles is what keeps us on the ladder toward happiness. When we find ourselves in the company of good friends, we thrive. We call each other out with an honesty that only our best friends can dish out. We encourage one another to achieve the highest state of happiness. We sustain one another in love, keeping our eyes forever fixed on the good of the other.

These positive relationships are being challenged by an increase in online communication. It would be in our best interest to lay down our phones and focus on developing friendships in real life that bring us closer to God.

---

[28] "6 Ways Social Media Is Ruining Our Friendships," *Relevant,* December 28, 2015, https://relevantmagazine.com/culture/tech/6-ways-social-media-ruining-our-friendships.
[29] *Illustrated London News,* June 6, 1931.

REFLECT

- Do you ever feel the "darkness" of phone use? How so?
- How often does your phone fall into the "urgent" list of your life?
- Do you spend more time interacting with friends and family via social media or text than in real life?
- Has your ability or motivation to interact with others face-to-face changed since you began this retreat?
- Do you consider yourself a good friend? Do you have someone in your life you would consider to be a good friend?

PRAY

God, you have chosen me to be your child. As such, I am to be in this world and not of it. Thank you for placing friends in my life to help me grow in faith so that we can go on loving you by loving one another. May I always seek their happiness and help them understand that their true joy is found solely in you. Thank you for being my best friend. Amen.

DAY 20

The Power of Habit: You Are What You Do

We all desire to achieve the fullest potential of our personal excellence. It's getting there that's the problem. Whenever we need to get from point A to point B, everything in between is a mystery to us. We know we must make the journey, but that's about all we know. We're never sure that when we take the first step we will be willing to take the second. We're timid when it comes to the unknown and the unpredictable.

Fear is part of our DNA. The human brain has been wired for centuries to recognize that doing something out of the ordinary is risky. Cavemen knew that every time they left their dwelling they would either come back with dinner or become something else's dinner. Tribal members from the first communities would not dare venture off on their own to live a life of solitude, because doing so could result in their death. The earliest workers of the land knew that if they didn't follow the rhythms of the seasons, their crops wouldn't yield enough for them to survive. Every person in the history of the world improved their odds of remaining in good health and security when they maintained a healthy fear of risk and followed the norms of their times.

Today, the norms for social behavior and physical survival have changed significantly due to advancements in technology. The habits we have formed in order to "fit in" with our communities and "thrive" as a society have gone digital. We are becoming lost in the labyrinth of this man-made environment.

Justin is a twenty-six-year-old freelance writer who spends most of his time in his apartment on his laptop. He rarely goes out because the group of friends he hung out with in college has since left town to pursue their own careers. That doesn't mean Justin has lost contact with his friends. On the contrary, he communicates with them almost every day on social media. In fact, Justin says that he talks with his friends more now than he ever did in college. He has more free time because he doesn't need to study, his working hours are flexible, and his friends are always online. When Justin feels lonely, he only needs to unlock his screen and scroll and instantly he feels "connected" to his friends by looking at their pictures, liking their posts, and sending and receiving messages.

Gloria is no different. She moved to the United States from Chile when she was twenty-two. Now, at twenty-six, she keeps in touch with her family in Chile using social-media apps on her smartphone. On top of that, she runs her own digital marketing business which allows her to work from home with flexible hours so that she can spend more time with her children. Unfortunately, due to the demands of her job and the differences in time zones, she needs to be connected to her device constantly to answer calls, text clients, or to simply talk with her mother.

Justin's and Gloria's digital habits are today's norm. Everywhere you go, there are people with their heads looking down, peering into screens. Whether waiting in line at a fast-food restaurant or going to the park with their children, everyone has gotten into the habit of screen-gazing as their primary mode of connecting socially, escaping boredom, and even earning money.

There is nothing inherently wrong with that. As mentioned before, technology is not evil in itself. On the contrary, its benefits have the potential to far outweigh its disadvantages. People in Third World countries now can take online courses and graduate with degrees that will benefit their lives tremendously. Students can take digital field trips and view live events from all over the world right from their own classroom. Gloria can speak to her family. The possibilities for the good that technology can produce are endless!

However, the current state of screen usage also has the potential to become behavioral addiction. Since the studies of behavioral addictions are in their infancy, we are not sure whether device usage has had more positive or more negative effects on our lives. We are still learning which digital behaviors constitute addictions and which ones are actually helping us live happy, efficient, and, from a religious perspective, holy lives.

What we do know, however, is that our habits have changed significantly since the late 1990s due to the influence of technology.

Researchers from Kent State University studied associations between greater cellphone use and less physical activity. They highlighted that college students who used their phones for more than five hours a day tended to be less fit than those who used their phones for one-and-a-half hours per day.[30]

Another research group from the U.S. National Library of Medicine and the National Institutes of Health, published findings that people who used their phones at night suffered from a vast array of effects of sleep deprivation caused by excess phone usage during the evening and nighttime hours.[31]

Finally, the National Safety Council reports that every year 1.6 million car crashes occur due to drivers being distracted by their phones while operating their vehicle. To put that into perspective, one out of every four accidents that occur in the United States come as a result of cellphone use.[32]

Our habits make us who we are. When we develop behavioral systems around acts repeated over and over each day, we embrace

---

[30] "Kent State Study Looks at Cell Phone Use and Fitness in College Students," Kent State University, April 27, 2015, https://www.kent.edu/kent/news/success/kent-state-study-looks-cell-phone-use-and-fitness-college-students.
[31] "Evening Exposure to a Light-Emitting Diode (LED)-Backlit Computer Screen Affects Circadian Physiology and Cognitive Performance," NCBI, March 17, 2011, https://www.ncbi.nlm.nih.gov/pubmed/21415172.
[32] "Texting and Driving Accident Statistics," https://www.edgarsnyder.com/car-accident/cause-of-accident/cell-phone/cell-phone-statistics.html.

those acts as the definition of our existence. The painter who puts brush to canvas every day grows in his ability to blend shape and color and, if he does this constantly and consistently, becomes a master artist. The software developer who writes code day in and day out embraces the puzzle of digital design and, after he creates several programs, becomes known as a master developer. The basketball player who sacrifices her time and energy to train and shoot jump shots repeatedly in the proper form, run defensive drills, and works successfully with like-minded teammates, earns the title of champion when she lifts the finals trophy in the air.

You are what you do. Your habits define your acts. That's the power of habit.

REFLECT

- What habits define you?
- Are these habits healthy?
- When people think of you, do they place you into the category of screen addict because you are typically not available to them?
- Do you find that you are more inclined to use your device or to speak with people in the flesh?
- Is your device the most effective means available to support your life economically, socially, and spiritually?
- Do your digital habits overshadow your life habits?

PRAY

Father, I long for holiness and wisdom. I desire it with every ounce of my soul and know that the only way to attain such a valued treasure is through you, whom I should love above all things. Please, I beg you, replace my habits of distraction with habits of attraction to you in all I say, all I do, all I play, and all I view. I am yours and, therefore, forever new. Amen.

DAY 21

Detached: The New Normal

This is not the end. This is the beginning.

Twenty-one days ago, you began detaching from more than just your phone. Yes, you managed to limit your screen time to an all-time low, but, more importantly, you humbled your spirit to an all-time high. That is the paradox of Christian servitude — in giving you receive, in your weakness you are strong, in dying you live, and in becoming detached to all things of this world you become attached to the one who matters most: God.

This is what was meant when it was written, "Seek first his kingdom and his righteousness, and all these things shall be yours as well" (Mt 6:33). To know God is to know all things. To contemplate his majesty and mercy is to gain wisdom. To live as he lived — that is, detached — is to live a life of happiness and holiness.

But there's more. The very next verse after the one just mentioned reads: "Therefore do not be anxious about tomorrow, for tomorrow will be anxious for itself. Let the day's own trouble be sufficient for the day." Tomorrow you might fall back into the funnel cloud that is your tech addiction. Society will see it as normal, and you will feel right at home swiping and tapping your screen at the rhythm of everyone else around you. In fact, you'll likely experience a sense of withdrawal from connectivity. You'll feel the urge to check your email, play a quick game, or to watch a few videos. At some point, you will be triggered … again and again and again.

Here are the two words that teach you how you avoid those temptations: production and consumption.

I was once in a mall with my mom. I was about fourteen years old and had a growing obsession for hip-hop music. This did not impress my morally grounded Catholic mother in the least. While we were heading toward the checkout counter, I casually removed the CD I was hiding and placed it on the register. Mom immediately saw the parental advisory label and then asked, "What is this?" I told her it was an album I wanted to get and, without making a scene, she looked at me and said, "Garbage in. Garbage out."

Then, she did something surprising: she let me buy the CD. I listened to it for years and purchased several others like it. I became a student of rap music and, since I was a basketball player, found it everywhere I went. Music with foul lyrics were all over television, radio, locker rooms, weight rooms, and even playing during pregame warm-ups. The songs played over and over in my head until I began using most of the bad words in my daily vernacular. It wasn't until I used a swear word in front of one of my best friends that he said, "Dude, since when do you swear?"

That's when my mom's words hit me. Garbage in. Garbage out. I had become what I had consumed. I had become trash.

I went home and broke every CD that had immoral content and/or swear words. I "took out the trash," and although I always have the temptation to slip back, I've managed to steer myself toward only the notes and lyrics that will strengthen my soul, be it secular or religious music.

Your digital life can become a cesspool for the production and consumption of content. Every post you promote, every product you purchase, every image you view, and every article you read plays a pivotal role in defining who you are. As you produce and consume content, you need to be careful about how you let it affect you. Every time you unlock a device, you are making a decision to provide the web with the possibility of influencing your soul. The things you consume become the things you post, and you essentially become what you eat.

From here on you have two choices every time you gravitate toward your phone: You can use it for good or for worse. Using your phone can lead toward a happier, holier life, or it can lead toward anger, depression, and anxiety. You can extend your joy with the consumption and production of truth, goodness, and beauty; or you can waste it with games and apps that provide nothing to show for them. You can use your phone to build yourself up or break yourself down, to extend your knowledge or to dampen it, to strengthen your soul and journey bravely toward your heavenly homeland or to weaken your spirit and crawl downtrodden toward the highway to hell.

As for me, my "new normal" has led me to experience new success. Since I detached from my phone, I've spent time in contemplative prayer almost every morning, which has proved to be my anchor in a whirlwind of countless activities that range from raising my young family, running two online businesses, teaching full time, and spending every other possible moment with my gorgeous wife. I've limited my phone usage to about thirty minutes a day, most of which I use to take pictures of my kids and pray using a Liturgy of the Hours app.

I've also carved out more moments to dedicate to my passion, which is writing books. In order to maximize my time to research and concentrate on this work, I decided to get off all social media, which has proved to be the greatest factor in my ability to write well. I no longer have a mind that is fragmented by a sense that I am "missing out" on social-media feeds. On the contrary, I am free from the distraction and better able to focus on the things I love to do, the people I love to be around, and the God who has blessed me with a peace and clarity that I never thought possible as the owner of a smartphone.

Granted there are times when I miss seeing a good meme or pictures of my friend's vacation to Rome; but I wouldn't trade the memories I've made adventuring with my family, the day-to-day revelations, nor the time and freedom to express my soul through writing for anything in the world. To say the least, my "new normal" is way better than my technology-addiction days.

This isn't the end of your retreat. This is the beginning of the "new normal" that is your digital life. You have made it up the steep ladder of digital detachment to a place where all of your spiritual needs are met. God has met you there, and in his arms he carries with him the gifts of solitude, silence, contemplation, passion, mission, community, friendship, and love.

I congratulate you for making it this far. Know that God has much more in store for your life than this. You have merely finished the prologue of your story of salvation. I cannot wait to see how the rest of your chapters play out, especially that surprise ending when the main character finally gets to meet the Author of Life.

REFLECT

- How many minutes have you been on your phone today? Compare that number to before you first downloaded the monitoring app on days 1 and 2.
- What do you anticipate your "new normal" to look like regarding the use of your phone?
- What steps will you put into place to ensure that you are doing God's will for tomorrow and every day thereafter?

PRAY

My most holy Lord, today marks the beginning of my new life with you in a world with less distraction and more clarity. Temptations will come; deflect them. Pressures will mount; level them. I will fail; raise me up. Breathe into me the same life that you breathed into Adam, and fortify me with your grace so that

I may withstand the devil's lures and remain holy for your sake and the sake of all of your people. Amen.

EPILOGUE

I have great news! You just successfully sacrificed 21 days of your 365 days this year (366 if it is a leap year). That is equivalent to roughly 5.8 percent of the year. I like to think of that as a tithe of your time. God asks us to tithe our money by offering a certain amount of our yearly income ("tithe" traditionally means 10 percent) for the support of the Church. Why not do the same thing with your time? If you want to make the complete 10 percent, repeat this retreat twice every year. I recommend doing so during the first three weeks of Advent and the first three weeks of Lent, as both seasons have a penitential vibe to them. This do-it-yourself retreat is a perfect resource for preparing yourself for the birth of Our Lord on Christmas Day and his passion, death, and resurrection during the Triduum and Easter Sunday.

You are now free to reactivate your phone apps, and maybe even discover some more. Just remember that your phone is a tool to be used for your benefit and the flourishing of all humankind. It can make you more efficient, more intelligent, and can even help you evangelize the world and advance God's kingdom. But it can also distract you to the point of addiction, which can result in disharmony with your work-life balance, your friendships, your family dynamics, and your relationship with God.

You are now probably feeling pretty happy about your accomplishment. But I can guarantee you, in a few weeks' time you will experience the urge to distract yourself and return to nonefficient phone use. After all, this has become not only an acceptable lifestyle but the normal way of life for most of the nearly 3.5 billion people who own smartphones in today's world.

When you fall back into distractible ways, know that this book and I will be waiting to provide you with the kickstart needed to detach yourself from your phone's addictive clutches. May it be for you the twenty-one-step ladder that will help you rise up, dust yourself off, and climb again to the heights of knowing, loving, and serving God with all of your soul, all of your heart, all of your mind … and less of your phone.

Your brother,

T. J.

ACKNOWLEDGMENTS

First and foremost, I want to thank Jesus, Saint Mary, Saint Joseph, and Saint Dominic who, in their unique and profound ways, have taught me how to live a simple life in the digital age.

I also want to thank my wife and children for being the mirror through which I was finally able to see my technology addiction. Thank you for pulling me into the happier reality of your smiles, hugs, laughs, giggles, and joy, which I pray continue to go viral in the quietness of my heart forever.

I want to thank my mom, dad, and siblings who never needed a mobile device to be entertained or a distraction to keep them from living lives of heroic virtue. You are all saints in my book.

Thank you, Fr. Steve Cron, for hearing my same technology-addiction confession for nearly ten years. I would simply not be here without the advice you offered and the books you recommended.

Thank you to Dr. Peter Kreeft who read my initial manuscript and encouraged me through handwritten letters to pursue the publication of this book. I am eternally grateful for this kind gesture.

Thank you, Rebecca Willen, my editor, and all of the people at OSV who shared my excitement for this book's theme. With your help this book was molded into something great. I pray that through it we can bring more people to the threshold of truth.

About the Author

T. J. Burdick is the author of several books and articles on the Catholic faith. He writes and speaks on how to grow in holiness amidst the distractions and difficulties of the current age. He resides in Grand Rapids, Michigan, with his wife and four children. When he is not spending time with his family or writing books, you can find him teaching courses on the Catholic faith through the Dominican Institute (dominicaninstitute.com), an online learning platform that serves students of every age and ability.